INTEGRAL HEALING

Integral Healing

Compiled from the Works of
Sri Aurobindo and the Mother

SRI AUROBINDO ASHRAM
PONDICHERRY

First edition 2004
Second impression 2006

Rs 105
ISBN-10: 81-7058-774-3
ISBN-13: 978-81-7058-774-3

Lotus Press   :ion Department,
PO Box 325
Twin Lakes, WI 53181 USA   am.org
www.lotuspress.com   Pondicherry
lotuspress@lotuspress.com

The Mother 1950

Sri Aurobindo c. 1915

Contents

INTRODUCTION
YOGA, EVOLUTION AND THE HUMAN BODY

1. The Need for a New Consciousness   3
   The Struggle of Forces   3
   The Old Spirituality and the New   4

2. Yoga in the Modern World   5
   What Is Yoga?   5
   Synthesis of Yogic Methods   6
   The Method and Process of Integral Yoga   7
   Finding Your Own Way   10

3. Integral Yoga and the Body   11
   The Body-Mind and the True Nature of Matter   13
   Inner Transformation and the Physical Resistance   14
   Illness in Yoga   16

PART ONE
PSYCHOLOGICAL CAUSES OF ILLNESS

1. Disequilibrium of the Being   23
   Harmony and Disorder   25
   Types and Causes of Disequilibrium   26
   Interchange with the Environment   30
   Microbes: Their Origin and the Forces Behind Them   32
   Restoring the Equilibrium   35

2. Weakness of the Nervous Envelope   39
   How the Forces of Illness Attack   40
   Sensing and Repelling Attacks of Illness   42
   Psychological States and the Nervous Envelope   46

3. Wrong Thinking   48
    The Power of Thought   50
    The Mentality of the Cells   52

4. Fear   54
    Fear and Contagion   56
    Sanitation and Health   60
    Getting Rid of Fear   63

5. The Subconscient   67
    Recurrent Illnesses and the Subconscient   69
    Removing the Psychological Roots of Illness   71

PART TWO
CURE BY INNER MEANS

1. Use of the Will   75
    Action of the Will on the Body and the Subconscient   76
    Cultivating the Will   77
    The Power of Sincerity   78

2. Imagination and Faith   80
    The Secret of Coué's Method   82
    Faith, Mental Effort and the Body   83

3. Detaching the Mind   87
    Release from Subjection to the Body   88
    Mastery of Mind over Body   89

4. Neutralising Pain   92
    Eliminating the Mental Factor in Pain   94
    Cutting the Connection   95
    Going out of the Body   98
    Moving the Centre of Awareness   99
    Widening Oneself   100

5. Quietude and Peace   103
   Quieting the Mind   103
   Making Oneself Blank   106
   Bringing Peace into the Body   107

6. Change of Consciousness   109
   Consciousness, Mind and Body   110

7. The Psychic Being   113
   The Psychic Being and the Outer Consciousness   114
   Psychic Discernment and Physical Disorders   115
   Accidents and an Awakened Consciousness   117
   Experiences of the Inner Being   119
   The Decisive Change   122
   The Sense of Eternity   123

8. Secrets of the Body-Consciousness   125
   The Body and Its Masters   127
   Letting the Body Restore Its Balance   129
   The Certitude of Cure   130
   The Vibratory Process of an Illness   132
   A Shift in Consciousness   134
   The Body as the Expression of a Deeper Reality   135
   Three Steps to Heal All Disorder   137

PART THREE
CURE BY SPIRITUAL FORCE

1. Divine Grace   141
   Letting the Grace Work   144
   Faith in the Divine   145
   Psychic Faith and Integral Faith   146
   Faith and Effort   147
   Miracles of the Grace   148
   Divine Intervention   149

2. Spiritual Force   152
     The Efficacy of the Force for Cure   153
     Becoming Conscious of the Force   155

3. Receptivity and Resistance to the Force   158
     Quietude and Receptivity   159
     Increasing the Physical Receptivity   160
     Applying the Force from Outside the Body   162

4. Opening the Body-Consciousness   164
     Passivity and Inertia   165
     Overcoming the Subconscient Resistance   168
     The Need for Perseverance   169

5. The Call and the Response   172
     The Secret of Effective Prayer   174
     Surrendering Responsibility   176
     The Surrender of the Cells   178

PART FOUR

MEDICINE AND HEALING

1. Medical Treatment and the Body-Consciousness   183
     Physical Support for the Action of the Force   184
     Alternative Healing Systems   186
     Strong Drugs and Side-Effects   187
     Nature as Healer   189
     Medical Science and the Curative Power Within Us   190
     Diseases, Disorders and Doctors   191

2. Doctors and the Healing Power   195
     Choosing One's Doctor   195
     Qualities of a Doctor   196
     Yoga and the Practice of Medicine   197
     The Doctor as an Instrument of the Divine   200
     The Force, the Instrument and the Instrumentation   202

The Collaboration of the Patient 205
Curing "Incurable" Illnesses 206

3. Intuitive Diagnosis 209
   Mental Intuition and Yogic Intuition 212
   Prognostications 214

4. Spiritual Healing 217
   Use of Spiritual Force 217
   Methods and Conditions of Effective Healing 219
   Healing with the Hands 220
   Thought-Formations and Praying for Others 222

CONCLUSION
BEYOND ILLNESS AND HEALING

1. The Transformation of Suffering 229
   Suffering as an Opportunity for Growth 231
   Pain, Pleasure and the Delight of Existence 233

References 237
Glossary 243
Index 248

Preface

Integral Healing presents the insights of Sri Aurobindo and the Mother into the causes and cure of illness. This book of selections from their writings and talks examines the mechanism of illness primarily from a psychological point of view, taking into account the whole of our being including much that is beyond the range of our normal awareness. It explores how the hidden causes of physical disorders can be uprooted by discovering and utilising one's inner power and participating consciously in the accelerated evolutionary process known as Integral Yoga.

Integral Yoga is the spiritual path that was originally developed and taught by Sri Aurobindo and the Mother at Sri Aurobindo Ashram in Pondicherry, India. In this book, the central principles of Integral Yoga and its vision of the evolving relation between matter and Spirit are explained in Sri Aurobindo's and the Mother's words in the Introduction, "Yoga, Evolution and the Human Body".

Sri Aurobindo, the prophet of a higher evolution, envisaged this path of Yoga as leading eventually through a radical change of consciousness to a total freedom from illness and the possibility of physical immortality. With regard to the body and its present subjection to illness, he stated that "the aim of our yoga is not to find out the most efficient method of healing diseases so much as to change the entire consciousness — even the physical — in order that disease may not come at all. The entire being must be so transformed that disease becomes impossible."

Integral healing in its completeness implies such a transformation by which illness, suffering and death would become things of the past. But before an evolutionary leap carries us beyond human nature as we know it, there are practical ways to maintain physical as well as psychological equilibrium and deal with the challenges that illness may present. These are the main subject of this book.

The seriousness of the problem has to be recognised and no simple panacea can be expected. As is explained in Part Four, "Medicine and Healing", medical treatment according to mainstream or alternative systems has its place alongside the inner and spiritual methods that are discussed in Parts Two and Three, "Cure by Inner Means" and "Cure by Spiritual Force".

Illness, suffering and death have been unavoidable circumstances in the emergence of living and thinking beings in a world of inanimate matter. But at a certain point, the human consciousness begins to become aware of something within or beyond itself whose nature is self-existent peace and bliss. A potent new factor is then introduced. This higher reality has long been experienced in various aspects by mystics and practitioners of the disciplines that in India are grouped under the heading of Yoga. In these disciplines, however, spiritual liberation has often been pursued for its own sake with little regard for its relevance to material life.

On the other hand, there are forms of Yoga that have concerned themselves with the body, such as Hathayoga, which is now synonymous with "yoga" for most people. But these have tended to rely on techniques that are predominantly physical and inherently limited in their results, however powerful within those limits. The attempt of the Integral Yoga to bring a force from the highest spiritual plane into the depths of matter opens up a frontier whose exploration could alter the equation between consciousness and the body it inhabits, with incalculable implications for the future.

Both Sri Aurobindo and the Mother practised healing over a period of decades in the course of their spiritual work, besides being engaged in the process of transformation in their own bodies. On the basis of their extensive experience, they sometimes spoke about illness and healing — especially self-healing — but did not fully systematise their knowledge on this subject. What they wrote or said in various contexts has been compiled in this book and arranged in such a way as to bring out the coherence and comprehensiveness of their vision of the human whole, including their understanding of the body, its disorders and its limitless potential.

The selections included here have been reproduced from diverse sources, formal and informal, written and spoken, some originally in English and some translated from French. Readers may notice considerable variations in style and tone from one page to the next as they read passages from Sri Aurobindo's major works and the Mother's accounts of her experiences of cellular transformation interspersed with written or oral answers to the questions of children and advanced sadhaks, laymen and doctors. (These questions are printed in italics.) Such variations were unavoidable if the subject matter of the book was to be covered as completely as possible in Sri Aurobindo's and the Mother's own words (or a translation of them, in the case of the Mother's talks).

Naturally, material extracted from so many different contexts could not be organised with the rigorous logic of a book planned and written from the beginning on a specific topic. Part One, for example, "Psychological Causes of Illness", is not strictly confined to an analysis of causes as implied by the title, but anticipates the methods of curing illnesses discussed in Parts Two and Three. Nevertheless, the compilers have tried to make the structure of the book reflect as clearly as possible the main aspects of Sri Aurobindo's and the Mother's contribution to the understanding of illness and how it can be cured.

Each part is divided into several chapters and the chapters into sections with headings indicating principal ideas. Short selections are grouped under these headings and long passages are broken up by them into smaller units. In the former case, the name of Sri Aurobindo or the Mother is printed (in bold type) at the beginning of the series of selections from each of them under a particular heading; in the latter case, the name appears only at the beginning of the entire passage. References to the sources of the texts, as well as a glossary and index, are found at the end of the book.

It is hoped that *Integral Healing* will be of value not only to those who wish to cure or prevent illness on the spiritual path, but to all who are interested in the theory and practice of holistic approaches to healing.

Richard Hartz

Introduction

Yoga, Evolution
and the Human Body

We are at a moment of transition in the history of the earth. It is merely a moment in eternal time, but this moment is long compared to human life. Matter is changing in order to prepare itself for the new manifestation, but the human body is not plastic enough and offers resistance; this is why the number of disorders and even incomprehensible diseases is increasing and becoming a problem for medical science.

The remedy lies in union with the divine forces that are at work and a receptivity full of trust and peace which makes the task easier.[1]

The Mother

1

The Need for a New Consciousness

The Mother: One thing seems obvious, that humanity has reached a certain state of general tension — tension in effort, tension in action, tension even in daily life — with such an excessive hyperactivity, such a widespread agitation, that the human race as a whole seems to have come to a point where it must either break through the resistance and emerge into a new consciousness or else fall back into an abyss of darkness and inertia.

This tension is so complete and so widespread that something obviously has to break. It cannot go on in this way. We may take it as a sure sign of the infusion into matter of a new principle of force, consciousness, power, which by its very pressure is producing this acute state. Outwardly, we could expect the old methods used by Nature when she wants to bring about an upheaval; but there is a new characteristic, which of course is only visible in an elite, but even this elite is fairly widespread — it is not localised at one point, at one place in the world; we find traces of it in all countries, all over the world: the will to find a new, higher, progressive solution, an effort to rise towards a vaster, more comprehensive perfection. . . .

The Struggle of Forces

This struggle, this conflict between the constructive forces of the ascending evolution of a more and more perfect and divine realisation, and the more and more destructive, powerfully destructive forces — forces that are mad beyond all control — is more and more obvious, marked, visible, and it is a kind of race or struggle to see which will reach the goal first. It would seem that all the adverse, anti-divine forces, the forces of the vital world, have descended on the earth, are making use of it as their field of action, and that at the same time a new, higher, more powerful spiritual force has also descended on earth to bring it a new life. This makes the struggle more acute, more violent, more visible, but it seems also more definitive, and that is why we can hope to reach an early solution.

The Old Spirituality and the New

There was a time, not so long ago, when the spiritual aspiration of man was turned towards a silent, inactive peace, detached from all worldly things, a flight from life, precisely to avoid battle, to rise above the struggle, escape all effort; it was a spiritual peace in which, along with the cessation of all tension, struggle, effort, there ceased also suffering in all its forms, and this was considered to be the true and only expression of a spiritual and divine life. It was considered to be the divine grace, the divine help, the divine intervention. And even now, in this age of anguish, tension, hypertension, this sovereign peace is the best received aid of all, the most welcome, the solace people ask and hope for. For many it is still the true sign of a divine intervention, of divine grace.

In fact, no matter what one wants to realise, one must begin by establishing this perfect and immutable peace; it is the basis from which one must work; but unless one is dreaming of an exclusive, personal and egoistic liberation, one cannot stop there. There is another aspect of the divine grace, the aspect of progress which will be victorious over all obstacles, the aspect which will propel humanity to a new realisation, which will open the doors of a new world and make it possible not only for a chosen few to benefit by the divine realisation but for their influence, their example, their power to bring to the rest of mankind new and better conditions.[2]

2

Yoga in the Modern World

Sri Aurobindo: The world today presents the aspect of a huge cauldron of Medea in which all things are being cast, shredded into pieces, experimented on, combined and recombined either to perish and provide the scattered material of new forms or to emerge rejuvenated and changed for a fresh term of existence. Indian Yoga, in its essence a special action or formulation of certain great powers of Nature, itself specialised, divided and variously formulated, is potentially one of these dynamic elements of the future life of humanity. The child of immemorial ages, preserved by its vitality and truth into our modern times, it is now emerging from the secret schools and ascetic retreats in which it had taken refuge and is seeking its place in the future sum of living human powers and utilities. But it has first to rediscover itself, bring to the surface the profoundest reason of its being in that general truth and that unceasing aim of Nature which it represents, and find by virtue of this new self-knowledge and self-appreciation its own recovered and larger synthesis. . . .

What Is Yoga?

In the right view both of life and of Yoga all life is either consciously or subconsciously a Yoga. For we mean by this term a methodised effort towards self-perfection by the expression of the secret potentialities latent in the being and — highest condition of victory in that effort — a union of the human individual with the universal and transcendent Existence we see partially expressed in man and in the Cosmos. But all life, when we look behind its appearances, is a vast

Yoga of Nature who attempts in the conscious and the sub-conscious to realise her perfection in an ever-increasing ex-pression of her yet unrealised potentialities and to unite herself with her own divine reality. In man, her thinker, she for the first time upon this Earth devises self-conscious means and willed arrangements of activity by which this great purpose may be more swiftly and puissantly attained. Yoga, as Swami Vivekananda has said, may be regarded as a means of com-pressing one's evolution into a single life or a few years or even a few months of bodily existence. A given system of Yoga, then, can be no more than a selection or a compression, into narrower but more energetic forms of intensity, of the general methods which are already being used loosely, largely, in a leisurely movement, with a profuser apparent waste of mate-rial and energy but with a more complete combination by the great Mother in her vast upward labour.

Synthesis of Yogic Methods

It is this view of Yoga that can alone form the basis for a sound and rational synthesis of Yogic methods. For then Yoga ceases to appear something mystic and abnormal which has no relation to the ordinary processes of the World-Energy or the purpose she keeps in view in her two great movements of subjective and objective self-fulfilment; it reveals itself rather as an intense and exceptional use of powers that she has al-ready manifested or is progressively organising in her less ex-alted but more general operations.

Yogic methods have something of the same relation to the customary psychological workings of man as has the scien-tific handling of the force of electricity or of steam to their normal operations in Nature. And they, too, like the opera-tions of Science, are formed upon a knowledge developed and confirmed by regular experiment, practical analysis and con-stant result. . . .

But as in physical knowledge the multiplication of scientific processes has its disadvantages, as that tends, for instance, to develop a victorious artificiality which overwhelms our natural human life under a load of machinery and to purchase certain forms of freedom and mastery at the price of an increased servitude, so the preoccupation with Yogic processes and their exceptional results may have its disadvantages and losses. The Yogin tends to draw away from the common existence and lose his hold upon it; he tends to purchase wealth of spirit by an impoverishment of his human activities, the inner freedom by an outer death. If he gains God, he loses life, or if he turns his efforts outward to conquer life, he is in danger of losing God. . . . No synthesis of Yoga can be satisfying which does not, in its aim, reunite God and Nature in a liberated and perfected human life or, in its method, not only permit but favour the harmony of our inner and outer activities and experiences in the divine consummation of both. For man is precisely that term and symbol of a higher Existence descended into the material world in which it is possible for the lower to transfigure itself and put on the nature of the higher and the higher to reveal itself in the forms of the lower.

The Method and Process of Integral Yoga

. . . It is always through something in the lower that we must rise into the higher existence, and the schools of Yoga each select their own point of departure or their own gate of escape. . . . But the normal action of Nature in us is an integral movement in which the full complexity of all our elements is affected by and affects all our environments. The whole of life is the Yoga of Nature. The Yoga that we seek must also be an integral action of Nature, and the whole difference between the Yogin and the natural man will be this, that the Yogin seeks to substitute in himself for the integral action of the lower Nature working in and by ego and division the integral action of the higher Nature working in and by God and unity. If indeed our aim be only an escape from the world to God, synthesis is unnecessary and a waste of time; for then our sole practical aim must be to find out one path out of the thousand that lead to God, one shortest possible of short cuts, and not to linger exploring different paths that end in the same goal. But if our aim be a transformation of our integral being into the terms of God-existence, it is then that a synthesis becomes necessary.

The method we have to pursue, then, is to put our whole conscious being into relation and contact with the Divine and to call Him in to transform our entire being into His. . . . The divine and all-knowing and all-effecting descends upon the limited and obscure, progressively illumines and energises the whole lower nature and substitutes its own action for all the terms of the inferior human light and mortal activity.

In psychological fact this method translates itself into the progressive surrender of the ego with its whole field and all its apparatus to the Beyond-ego with its vast and incalculable but always inevitable workings. . . .

There are three outstanding features of this action of the higher when it works integrally on the lower nature. In the first place, it does not act according to a fixed system and succession as in the specialised methods of Yoga, but with a sort of free, scattered and yet gradually intensive and purposeful working determined by the temperament of the individual in whom it operates, the helpful materials which his nature offers and the obstacles which it presents to purification and perfection. In a sense, therefore, each man in this path has his own method of Yoga. Yet are there certain broad lines of working common to all which enable us to construct not indeed a routine system, but yet some kind of Shastra or scientific method of the synthetic Yoga.

Secondly, the process, being integral, accepts our nature such as it stands organised by our past evolution and without rejecting anything essential compels all to undergo a divine change. Everything in us is seized by the hands of a mighty Artificer and transformed into a clear image of that which it now seeks confusedly to present. In that ever-progressive experience we begin to perceive how this lower manifestation is constituted and that everything in it, however seemingly deformed or petty or vile, is the more or less distorted or imperfect figure of some element or action in the harmony of the divine Nature. . . .

Thirdly, the divine Power in us uses all life as the means of this integral Yoga. Every experience and outer contact with our world-environment, however trifling or however disastrous, is used for the work, and every inner experience, even to the most repellent suffering or the most humiliating fall, becomes a step on the path to perfection.[3]

What is one to do to prepare oneself for the Yoga?

The Mother: To be conscious, first of all. We are conscious of only an insignificant portion of our being; for the most part we are unconscious. It is this unconsciousness that keeps us down to our unregenerated nature and prevents change and transformation in it. It is through unconsciousness that the undivine forces enter into us and make us their slave. You are to be conscious of yourself, you must awake to your nature and movements, you must know why and how you do things or feel or think them; you must understand your motives and impulses, the forces, hidden and apparent, that move you; in fact, you must, as it were, take to pieces the entire machinery of your being. Once you are conscious, it means that you can distinguish and sift things, you can see which are the forces that pull you down and which help you on. And when you know the right from the wrong, the true from the false, the divine from the undivine, you are to act strictly up to your knowledge; that is to say, resolutely reject one and accept the other. The duality will present itself at every step and at every step you will have to make your choice. You will have to be patient and persistent and vigilant — "sleepless", as the adepts say; you must always refuse to give any chance whatever to the undivine against the divine.[4]

Finding Your Own Way

The Mother: To cling to what you believe you know, to cling to what you feel, to cling to what you love, to cling to your habits, to cling to your so-called needs, and to cling to the world as it is, that is what binds you. You must undo all that, one thing after another. Undo all the ties. And it has been said thousands of times and people go on doing the same thing... Even those who are most eloquent and preach it to others, c-l-i-n-g — they cling to their way of seeing, to their way of feeling, their habit of progress, which seems for them the only one.

No more bonds — free, free. Always ready to change everything, except one thing: to aspire, this thirst.

I understand very well, there are people who do not like the idea of a "Divine", . . . but you don't need that! — the "something" you need, the Light you need, the Love you need, the Truth you need, the supreme Perfection you need — and that is all. The formulas. . . the fewer formulas the better. But this: a need, which *the* Thing alone can satisfy — nothing else, no half-measures, only that. And then, go! ... Your way will be your way, that has no importance — whatever the way, it doesn't matter, even the extravagances of the modern American youth can be a way, that has no importance.[5]

3

Integral Yoga and the Body

Sri Aurobindo: I have never had any hesitation in the use of a spiritual force for all legitimate purposes including the maintenance of health and physical life in myself and in others. . . . I put a value on the body first as an instrument, *dharma-sādhana*, or, more fully, as a centre of manifested personality in action, a basis of spiritual life and activity as of all life and activity upon the earth, but also because for me the body as well as the mind and life is a part of the Divine Whole, a form of the Spirit and therefore not to be disregarded or despised as something incurably gross and incapable of spiritual realisation or of spiritual use. Matter itself is secretly a form of the Spirit and has to reveal itself as that, can be made to wake to consciousness and evolve and realise the Spirit, the Divine within it. In my view the body as well as the mind and life has to be spiritualised or, one may say, divinised so as to be a fit instrument and receptacle for the realisation of the Divine.[6]

The way of yoga followed here has a different purpose from others, — for its aim is not only to rise out of the ordinary ignorant world-consciousness into the divine consciousness, but to bring the supramental power of that divine consciousness down into the ignorance of mind, life and body, to transform them, to manifest the Divine here and create a divine life in Matter.[7]

These are some of the effects of the descent of higher Consciousness into the most physical. It brings light, consciousness, force, Ananda into the cells and all the physical movements. The body becomes conscious and vigilant and performs the right movements, obeying the higher will or else automatically by the force of the consciousness that has come into it. It becomes more possible to control the functions of the body and set right anything that is wrong, to deal with illness and pain, etc. A greater control comes over the actions of the body and even over happenings to it from outside. . . . The body becomes a more effective instrument for work. It becomes possible to minimise fatigue. Peace, happiness, strength, lightness come in the whole physical system.[8]

As a result of this new relation between the Spirit and the body, the gnostic evolution will effectuate the spiritualisation, perfection and fulfilment of the physical being; it will do for the body as for the mind and life. Apart from the obscurity, frailties and limitations, which this change will overcome, the body-consciousness is a patient servant and can be in its large reserve of possibilities a potent instrument of the individual life, and it asks for little on its own account: what it craves for is duration, health, strength, physical perfection, bodily happiness, liberation from suffering, ease. . . . When the gnostic Force can act in the body, these things can be established; for their opposites come from a pressure of external forces on the physical mind, on the nervous and material life, on the body-organism, from an ignorance that does not know how to meet these forces or is not able to meet them rightly or with power, and from some obscurity, pervading the stuff of the physical consciousness and distorting its responses, that reacts to them in a wrong way.[9]

The Body-Mind and the True Nature of Matter

Sri Aurobindo: There is too an obscure mind of the body, of the very cells, molecules, corpuscles. Haeckel, the German materialist, spoke somewhere of the will in the atom, and recent science, dealing with the incalculable individual variation in the activity of the electrons, comes near to perceiving that this is not a figure but the shadow thrown by a secret reality. This body-mind is a very tangible truth; owing to its obscurity and mechanical clinging to past movements and facile oblivion and rejection of the new, we find in it one of the chief obstacles to permeation by the supermind Force and the transformation of the functioning of the body. On the other hand, once effectively converted, it will be one of the most precious instruments for the stabilisation of the supramental Light and Force in material Nature.[10]

The Mother: There is a consciousness in the cells: it is what we call the "body consciousness" and it is wholly bound up with the body. This consciousness has much difficulty in changing, because it is under the influence of the collective suggestion which is absolutely opposed to the transformation. So one has to struggle with this collective suggestion, not only with the collective suggestion of the present, but with the collective suggestion which belongs to the earth-consciousness as a whole, the terrestrial human consciousness which goes back to the earliest formation of man. That has to be overcome before the cells can be spontaneously aware of the Truth, of the Eternity of matter.[11]

As you descend into that domain, the domain of the cells, even of the very constitution of the cells, how it seems less heavy! This sort of heaviness of Matter disappears — it begins again to be fluid, vibrant. This would tend to prove that the heaviness, thickness, inertia, immobility, is something *added*, it is not a quality essential to. . . it is the false Matter, that which we think and feel, but not Matter itself, as it is.[12]

Inner Transformation and the Physical Resistance

The Mother: The force that comes down into one who is doing Yoga and helps him in his transformation, acts along many different lines and its results vary according to the nature that receives it and the work to be done. First of all, it hastens the transformation of all in the being that is ready to be transformed. If he is open and receptive in his mind, the mind, touched by the power of Yoga, begins to change and progress swiftly. There may be the same rapidity of change in the vital consciousness if that is ready, or even in the body. But in the body the transforming power of Yoga is operative only to a certain degree; for the receptivity of the body is limited. The most material plane of the universe is still in a condition in which receptivity is mixed with a large amount of resistance. But rapid progress in one part of the being which is not followed by an equivalent progress in other parts produces a disharmony in the nature, a dislocation somewhere; and wherever or whenever this dislocation occurs, it can translate itself into an illness. The nature of the illness depends upon the nature of the dislocation. One kind of disharmony affects the mind and the disturbance it produces may lead even as far as insanity; another kind affects the body and may show itself as fever or prickly heat or any other greater or minor disorder.

On one side, the action of the forces of Yoga hastens the movement of transformation of the being in those parts that are ready to receive and respond to the power that is at work upon it. Yoga, in this way, saves time. The whole world is in a process of progressive transformation; if you take up the discipline of Yoga, you speed up in yourself this process. The work that would require years in the ordinary course, can be done by Yoga in a few days and even in a few hours. But it is your inner consciousness that obeys this accelerating impulse; for the higher parts of your being readily follow the swift and concentrated movement of Yoga and lend themselves more easily to the continuous adjustment and adaptation that it necessitates. The body, on the other hand, is ordinarily dense, inert and apathetic. And if you have in this part something that is not responsive, if there is a resistance here, the reason is that the body is incapable of moving as quickly as the rest of the being. It must take time, it must walk at its own pace as it does in ordinary life. What happens is as when grown-up people walk too fast for children in their company; they have to stop at times and wait till the child who is lagging behind comes up and overtakes them. This divergence between the progress in the inner being and the inertia of the body often creates a dislocation in the system, and that manifests itself as an illness. This is why people who take up Yoga frequently begin by suffering from some physical discomfort or disorder. That need not happen if they are on their guard and careful. Or if there is a greater and unusual receptivity in the body, then too they escape. But an unmixed receptivity making the physical parts closely follow the pace of the inner transformation is hardly possible, unless the body has already been prepared in the past for the processes of Yoga.

In the ordinary life of man a progressive dislocation is the rule. The mental and the vital beings of man follow as best they can the movement of the universal forces, and the stream of the world's inner transformation and evolution carries them a certain way; but the body bound to the law of the most material nature, moves very slowly. After some years, seventy or eighty, a hundred or two hundred, — and that is perhaps the maximum, — the dislocation is so serious that the outer being falls to pieces. The divergence between the demand and the answer, the increasing inability and irresponsiveness of the body, brings about the phenomenon of death. By Yoga the inner transformation that is in slow constant process in the creation is rendered more intense and rapid, but the pace of the outer transformation remains almost the same as in ordi-

nary life. As a result, the disharmony between the inner and
the outer being in one who is doing Yoga tends to be all the
greater, unless precautions are taken and a protection secured
that will help the body to follow the inner march as closely as
possible. Even then it is the very nature of the body to hold
you back. It is for this reason that to many we are obliged to
say, "Do not pull, do not hurry; you must give your body
time to follow."[13]

Illness is always a fall back into inconscience through the incapacity to sustain the movement of transformation. And death
is the same thing — it is the same thing, only a little more
total.[14]

Every disease has its own vibratory mode; it represents a whole
field of vibrations to be corrected. It is the *exact* measure of
what in Matter resists the divine Influence — the exact measure, to the atom.[15]

Illness in Yoga

The Mother: There is an aspiration within you (I am speaking
now of people who do yoga or at any rate know what the
spiritual life is and try to walk on the path), within you there
is a part of the being — either mental or vital or something
even physical — that has understood well, has much aspiration, its special aptitudes, that receives the forces well and is
making good progress. And then there are others that cannot,
others still that don't want to (that of course is very bad), but
there are yet others that want to very much but cannot, do
not have the capacity, are not ready. So there is something
that rises upward and something that does not move. That

causes a terrible imbalance. And usually this translates itself into some illness or other, for you are in such a state of inner tension between something that cannot or something that clings, that does not want to move and something else that wants to: that produces a frightful unease and the result usually is an illness. . . .

You do the yoga according to your capacity. You have been told: "Open yourself, you will receive the Force." You have been told: "Have faith, be of goodwill and you will be protected." And indeed you are bathed in the Consciousness, bathed in the Force, bathed in the Protection and to the extent you have faith and open yourself, you receive all that, and it helps you to keep well and reject little inner disturbances and re-establish order when they come, to protect yourself against small attacks or accidents which might have happened. But if somewhere in your being — either in your body or in your vital or mind, in several parts or even in a single one — there is an incapacity to receive the descending Force, this acts like a grain of sand in a machine. You know, a fine machine working quite well with everything going all right, and you put into it just a little sand (nothing much, only a grain of sand), suddenly everything is damaged and the machine stops. Well, just a little lack of receptivity somewhere, something that is unable to receive the Force, that is completely shut up (when one looks at it, it becomes like a little dark spot somewhere, a tiny thing hard as a stone: the Force cannot enter into it, it refuses to receive it — either it cannot or it will not) and immediately that produces a great imbalance; and this thing that was moving upward, that was blooming so wonderfully, finds itself sick, and sometimes just when you were in a normal equilibrium; you were in good health, everything was fine, you had nothing to complain about. One day when you had grasped a new idea, received a new stimulus, when you had a great aspiration and received a great force and had a marvellous experience, a beautiful experience opening inner doors, giving you a knowledge you did not have before; you were sure everything was going to go well.... The next day, you are taken ill. So you say: "Still that? It is impossible! That should not happen." But it was quite simply what I have just said: a grain of sand. There was something that could not receive; immediately it brings about a disequilibrium. Even though very small it is enough, and you fall ill.[16]

But are not illnesses sometimes the result of microbes and not a part of the movement of the Yoga?

Where does Yoga begin and where does it end? Is not the whole of your life Yoga? The possibilities of illness are always there in your body and around you; you carry within you or there swarm about you the microbes and germs of every disease. How is it that all of a sudden you succumb to an illness which you did not have for years? You will say it is due to a "depression of the vital force". But from where does the depression come? It comes from some disharmony in the being, from a lack of receptivity to the divine forces. When you cut yourself off from the energy and light that sustain you, then there is this depression, there is created what medical science calls a "favourable ground" and something takes advantage of it. It is doubt, gloominess, lack of confidence, a selfish turning back upon yourself that cuts you off from the light and divine energy and gives the attack this advantage. It is this that is the cause of your falling ill and not microbes.[17]

Are illnesses tests in the Yoga?

Tests? Not at all.

You are given an illness purposely to make you progress? Surely it is not like that. That is, you may turn it round and say that there are people whose aspiration is so constant, whose goodwill is so total that whatever happens to them they take as a trial on the path to make progress. I knew people who, whenever they fell ill, took it as a proof of the Divine Grace to help them to progress. They told themselves: it is a good sign, I am going to find out the cause of my illness and make the necessary progress. I knew a few of this kind and they advanced magnificently. There are others, on the contrary, who, far from making use of it, let themselves fall flat on the ground. . . . But the true attitude when one is ill, is to say: "There is something wrong; I am going to see what it is."[18]

Part One

Psychological Causes of Illness

An illness of the body is always the outer expression and translation of a disorder, a disharmony in the inner being; unless this inner disorder is healed, the outer cure cannot be total and permanent.[1]

The Mother

1

Disequilibrium of the Being

The Mother: If the whole being could simultaneously advance in its progressive transformation, keeping pace with the inner march of the universe, there would be no illness, there would be no death. But it would have to be literally the whole being integrally from the highest planes, where it is more plastic and yields in the required measure to transforming forces, down to the most material, which is by nature rigid, stationary, refractory to any rapid remoulding change.

There are certain regions which offer a much stronger resistance than others to the action of the Yogic forces, and the illnesses affecting them are harder to cure. They are those parts that belong to the most material layers of the being, and the illnesses that pertain to them, as, for instance, skin diseases or bad teeth. Sri Aurobindo spoke once of a Yogi who, still enjoying robust health and a magnificent physique, had been living for nearly a century on the banks of the Narmada. Offered by a disciple medicine for a toothache, he observed, in refusing, that one tooth had given him trouble for the last two hundred years. This Yogi had secured so much control over material nature as to live two hundred years, but in all that time he had not been able to conquer a toothache.

Some of the diseases which are considered most dangerous are the easiest to cure; some that are considered as of very little importance can offer the most obstinate resistance.[2]

Each spot of the body is symbolical of an inner movement; there is there a world of subtle correspondences. . . . The particular place in the body affected by an illness is an index to the nature of the inner disharmony that has taken place. It points to the origin, it is a sign of the cause of the ailment. It reveals too the nature of the resistance that prevents the whole being from advancing at the same high speed. It indicates the treatment and the cure. If one could perfectly understand where the mistake is, find out what has been unreceptive, open that part and put the force and the light there, it would be possible to re-establish in a moment the harmony that has been disturbed and the illness would immediately go.

The origin of an illness may be in the mind; it may be in the vital; it may be in any of the parts of the being. One and the same illness may be due to a variety of causes; it may spring in different cases from different sources of disharmony. And there may be too an appearance of illness where there is no real illness at all. In that case, if you are sufficiently conscious, you will see that there is just a friction somewhere, some halting in the movement, and by setting it right you will be cured at once. This kind of malady has no truth in it, even when it seems to have physical effects. It is half made up of imagination and has not the same grip on matter as a true illness.

In short, the sources of an illness are manifold and intricate; each can have a multitude of causes, but always it indicates where is the weak part in the being.[3]

In reality illness is only a disequilibrium; if then you are able to establish another equilibrium, this disequilibrium disappears. An illness is simply, always, in every case, even when the doctors say that there are microbes — in every case, a disequilibrium in the being: a disharmony among the various functions, a disharmony among the forces.

This is not to say that there are no microbes: there are, there are many more microbes than are now known. But that is not why you are ill, for they are always there. It happens that they are always there and for days they do nothing to you and then all of a sudden, one day, one of them gets hold of you and makes you ill — why? Simply because the resistance was not as it usually is, because there was some disequilibrium in some part, the functioning was not normal. But if, by an inner power, you can re-establish the equilibrium, then that is the end of it, there is no more difficulty, the disequilibrium disappears.

There is no other way to cure people. It is simply when you see the disequilibrium and are capable of re-establishing equilibrium that one is cured.[4]

Harmony and Disorder

Are illnesses and accidents the result of something bad one has thought or done, of a fall in one's consciousness? If the cause is a mistake one has made, how can one find out what it is?

The Mother: It has nothing to do with *punishment*, it is the natural and normal consequence of an error, shortcoming or fault which necessarily has consequences. Actually, everything in the world is a question of equilibrium or disequilibrium, of harmony or disorder. Vibrations of harmony attract and encourage harmonious events; vibrations of disequilibrium create, as it were, a disequilibrium in circumstances (illnesses, accidents, etc.). This may be collective or individual, but the principle is the same — and so is the remedy: to cultivate in oneself order and harmony, peace and equilibrium by surrendering unreservedly to the Divine Will.[5]

Let us say a group of cells break down; for some reason or other (there are countless reasons), they submit to disorder — obey the disorder — and a particular point becomes "sick" according to the ordinary view of illnesses. But that intrusion of disorder makes itself felt everywhere, it has repercussions everywhere: wherever there is a point that is weaker or less resistant to attack, it manifests. Take someone who is in the habit of getting a headache, or toothache, or a cough, or neuralgic pains, whatever, a host of little things like that, which come and go, increase and decrease. But if there is an attack of disorder somewhere, a serious attack, all these little troubles reappear instantly, here, there, there... It is a fact I have observed. And the opposite movement follows the same pattern: if you are able to bring to the attacked spot the true Vibration — the Vibration of order and harmony — and you stop the disorder... all the other things are put back in order, as if automatically.

And it is not through contagion; it is not that, for instance, the blood carries the illness here or there, that isn't it: it is... almost like a spirit of imitation.

But the truth is that the Harmony that keeps everything together has been attacked, it has succumbed, and so everything is disrupted, each thing in its own way and according to its own habit. . . .

It is something I have observed on the level of the body's cells hundreds and hundreds of times. And then, you no longer have at all that mental impression of one disorder added to another, which makes the problem more difficult — that isn't it at all, it is... if you get to the centre, all the rest will be naturally restored to order. And that is a fact: if order is restored at the centre of disorder, everything follows naturally, without your paying it any special attention.[6]

Types and Causes of Disequilibrium

The Mother: I have told you . . . that all illnesses, all, whatever they may be (I would add even accidents), come from a break in equilibrium. That is, if all your organs, all the members and parts of your body are in harmony with one another, you are in perfect health. But if there is the slightest imbalance anywhere, immediately you get either just a little ill or quite ill, even very badly ill, or else you have an accident. It is always when there is an inner imbalance.

But then, to the equilibrium of the body, you must add the equilibrium of the vital and the mind. For you to be able to do all kinds of things with immunity, without any accident happening to you, you must have a triple equilibrium — mental, vital, physical — and not only in each of the parts, but also in the three parts in their mutual relations.... If you have done a little mathematics, you should have been taught how many combinations that makes and what a difficult thing it means! There lies the key to the problem. For the combinations are innumerable, and consequently the causes of illness too are innumerable, the causes of accidents also are innumerable. Still, we are going to try to classify them so that we may understand.

First of all, from the point of view of the body — just the body — there are two kinds of disequilibrium: functional and organic. I do not know if you are aware of the difference between the two; but you have organs and then you have all the parts of your body: nerves, muscles, bones and all the rest. Now, if an organ by itself is in disequilibrium, it is an organic disequilibrium, and you are told: that organ is ill or perhaps it is badly formed or it is not normal or an accident has occurred to it. But it is the organ that is ill. Yet the organ may be in a very good condition, all your organs may be in a very good condition, but there is still an illness as they do not function properly: there is a lack of balance in the functioning. . . . Then you have an illness due to functional imbalance, not organic imbalance.

Generally, illnesses due to functional imbalance are cured much more quickly and easily than the others. The others are a little more serious. Sometimes they become very grave. So there are already two domains to see and know, but if you have a little knowledge of your body and the habit of observing its working, you can know what kind of imbalance you have.

Most often when you are young and leading a normal life,

the imbalance is purely functional. There are only a few unfortunate people who for one reason or another have suffered
from an accident or disequilibrium before their birth, these
carry with them something that is much more difficult to cure
(not that it is incurable; in theory, there is nothing incurable,
but it becomes more difficult).

Now, what are the causes of this imbalance, whatever it
may be? As I told you just now, the causes are innumerable;
because, first of all, there are all the inner causes, that is, those
personal to you, and then all the external causes, those that
come to you from outside. That makes two major categories.

The internal causes:

We said: you have a brain, lungs, a heart, a stomach, a
liver, etc. If each one does its duty and works normally and if
all move together in harmony at the required moment and in
the right way (note that it is very complicated; if you had to
think of all that, I am afraid things would not go very well all
the time! — fortunately, it does not depend on our conscious
thought), but say they are in good harmony with one another,
good friends, in perfect agreement, and each one is fulfilling
its task, its movement at the right time, in step with the rest,
neither too soon nor too late, neither too fast nor too slow, in
short, everyone is fine, you are marvellously well! Suppose
now that one of them, for some reason or other, happens to
be in a bad mood: it does not work with the necessary energy
at the required moment, it is more or less on strike. Do not
believe that it will be ill by itself: the whole system will go
wrong and you will feel altogether unwell. And if, unfortunately, there is a vital imbalance, that is, a disappointment or
too violent an emotion or too strong a passion or something
else upsetting your vital, that comes and aggravates it. And if
in addition your thoughts roam about and you begin to have
dark ideas and formulate frightful things and make catastrophic formations, then after that you are sure to fall quite
ill.... You see the complication, don't you, just a tiny thing can
go wrong and this through an inner contagion can lead to
something very serious. So what is important is to control

things immediately. One must be conscious, conscious of the working of one's organs, aware of any that is not behaving properly, telling it immediately what is to be done to set itself right. . . . Suppose, for example, your heart begins to throb madly; then you must make it calm, you tell it that this is not the way to act, and at the same time (just to help it) you take in long, very regular rhythmic breaths, that is, the lungs become the mentor of the heart and teach it how to work properly. And so on. I could give you countless examples.

All right. We say then that there is imbalance between the different parts of the being, disharmony in their working. That is what I have just told you. And then there are internal conflicts. These are quarrels. There are internal quarrels among the different parts of yourself. Suppose there is an organ (it happens very often) that needs rest and there is another that wants action, and both at the same time. How are you going to handle it? They begin to quarrel. If you do what one wants, the other protests! And so you have to find a middle term to put them in harmony. And then, at times, if to the physical you add the vital and mental . . . you have a battlefield, and this battlefield can become the cause of all possible illnesses. They fight violently. One wants something, the other does not, they quarrel and you are in a kind of internal whirlwind. That can give you a fever (it usually does) or else you are seized by an inner shivering and you have no more control. For the most important of all causes of bodily illness is that the body begins to get restless; it trembles and the trembling increases more and more, more and more and you feel that you will never be able to re-establish the balance, it eludes you. Then in that case you must know what the dispute is about, the reason for the dispute and find out how to reconcile the people within you. . . .

You see there are reasons! — many reasons, numberless reasons. For all these things combine in an extraordinarily complex way, and in order to know, in order to be able to cure an illness, one must find out its cause, not its microbe. For it happens that (excuse me, I hope there are no doctors here!), it happens that when microbes are there, they find out magnificent remedies to kill the microbes, but these remedies cure some and make others much worse! Nobody knows why.... Perhaps I know why. Because the illness had another cause than the purely physical one; there was something else, this was only an outer expression of a different disorder; and unless you touch that, discover that disorder, you will never be able to prevent the illness from coming. . . .

Interchange with the Environment

Thus we have seen in brief, very rapidly, all the internal causes. Now there are external causes that come and complicate things.

If you were in a perfectly harmonious environment where everything was in a state of total and perfect goodwill, then evidently you could lay the blame only on yourself. But the difficulties inside are also outside. You can, to a certain extent, establish an inner equilibrium, but you live in surroundings full of disequilibriums. Unless you shut yourself up in an ivory tower (which is not only difficult, but not always advisable), you are obliged to receive what comes from outside. You give and you receive; you breathe in and absorb. So there is a mixture and that is why one can say that everything is contagious, for you live in a state of ceaseless vibrations. You emit your own vibrations and you receive in turn the vibrations of others, and these vibrations are of a very complex nature. There are again (we shall say to simplify the terminology) mental vibrations, vital vibrations, physical vibrations, and many others. You give, you receive, you give, you receive. It is a perpetual play. Even granting that there is no bad will, there is necessarily a contagion. And as I was saying just now, all is contagious, everything. You are looking at the result of an accident: you absorb a certain vibration. And if you are ultra-sensitive and on top of that are afraid or disgusted (which is the same thing, disgust is only a moral expression of a physical fear), the accident can be translated physically in your body. Naturally you will be told that it is people in a state of nervous instability who have such reactions. It is not quite like that. They are people with a kind of vital over-sensitivity, that is all. And it is not always a proof of inferiority, on the contrary! For as you progress spiritually, a certain hypersensitivity of the nerves develops and if your self-control does not increase along with your sensitivity, all kinds of untoward things may happen to you.

But that is not the only thing.

Unfortunately there is much bad will in the world; and among the different kinds of bad will there is the small kind that comes from ignorance and stupidity, there is the big kind that comes from wickedness, and there is the formidable kind that is the result of anti-divine forces. So all that is in the atmosphere (I am not telling you this to frighten you, for it is understood that one should fear nothing — but it is there all the same) and these things attack you, sometimes intentionally, sometimes unintentionally. Unintentionally, through other people: others are attacked, they don't know it, they pass it on without even being aware of it. They are the first victims. They pass the illness on to others. . . .

There are in the physical atmosphere, the earth-atmosphere, numerous small entities which you do not see, for your vision is too limited, but which move about in your atmosphere. Some of them are quite nice, others very wicked. Generally these little entities are produced by the disintegration of vital beings — they pullulate — and these form quite an unpleasant mass. There are some who do very nice things. I believe I told you the story of the little beings who tugged at my sari to tell me that the milk was about to boil and that I had to go and see that it did not boil over. But all of them are not so good. Some of them like to play ugly little tricks, wicked little pranks. And so most often it is they who are behind an accident. They like little accidents, they like the whole whirl of forces that gather round an accident: a lot of people, you know, it is very amusing! And then that gives them their food, because, in fact, they feed upon human vitality thrown out of the body by emotions and excitement. So they say: just a small accident, how nice, many accidents!

Microbes: Their Origin and the Forces Behind Them

Now, if there is a group of such small entities, they may clash with one another, because among themselves they do not have a very peaceful life: clashing with one another, fighting, destroying, demolishing each other. And that is the origin of microbes. They are forces of disintegration. But they continue to be alive even in their divided forms and this is the origin of germs and microbes. Therefore most microbes have behind them a bad will and that is what makes them so dangerous. And unless one knows the quality and kind of bad will and is capable of acting upon it, there is a ninety-nine percent chance of not finding the true and total remedy. The microbe is a very material expression of something living in a subtle physical world and that is why these very microbes . . . that are always around you, within you, for years together do not hurt you and then, all of a sudden, they make you ill.

There is another reason. It is that there is a disharmony, a receptivity of the being with regard to the adverse force which is the origin and support of the microbes. I will tell you a story . . . for it will give you an illustration.

I was in Japan. It was the beginning of January, 1919. It was the time when a terrible flu raged there, in the whole of Japan, which killed hundreds of thousands of people. It was one of those epidemics such as are rarely seen. In Tokyo, every day there were hundreds and hundreds of new cases. The disease followed this course: it lasted three days and on the third day the patient died. And people died in such large numbers that they could not even be cremated, you understand, it was impossible, there were too many of them. Or otherwise, if one did not die on the third day, at the end of seven days one was completely cured; a little exhausted, but all the same completely cured. There was a panic in the town, for epidemics are very rare in Japan. They are a very clean people, very careful and with a fine morale. Illnesses are very rare. But anyway it happened like that, as a catastrophe. There was a terrible fear. For example, people were seen walking about in the streets with a mask over the nose, a purifying mask so that the air they were breathing would not be full of the microbes of the disease. It was a general fear.... Now, it so happened that I was living with someone who never stopped pestering me: "But what is this disease? What is behind this disease?" What I was doing, you know, was simply to surround myself with my force, my protection so as not to catch it and I didn't think about it any more and continued doing my work. Nothing happened and I wasn't thinking about it. But constantly I heard: "What is this? Oh, I would like to know what is behind this disease. Can't you tell me what this disease is, why it is there?..." etc. One day I was called to the other end of town by a young woman whom I knew and who wished to introduce me to some friends or show me something (I don't remember now exactly what the reason was, but anyway I had to cross the whole city in a tram-car). And I was in the tram seeing these people with masks over their noses, and there was this constant fear in the atmosphere, and then there was this suggestion; I began to ask myself: "Really, what is this disease? What is behind this disease? What are the forces in this disease?..." I arrived at the house, I spent an hour there and left. And I returned home with a terrible fever. I had caught it. It came to you like that, without warning, instantaneously. Illnesses, illnesses from germs and microbes, generally take a few days in the system: they come, there is a little battle inside; you win or you lose. If you lose you catch the illness, it is not complicated. But here, you just receive a letter, open the envelope, hop! puff! The next minute you have the fever. Well, that evening I had a terrible fever. The doctor was called (it was not I who called him), the doctor was called and he told me: "I absolutely must give you this medicine." It was one of the best medicines for the fever, he had just a little (all their stocks were exhausted, everyone was taking it); he said: "I still have a few packets, I will give you some." "Please don't give it to me, I won't take it. Keep it for someone who has faith in it and will take it." He was quite disgusted: "It was no use my coming here." So I said: "Perhaps it was no use!" And I remained in my bed, with my fever, a violent fever. All the while I was asking myself: "What is this illness? Why is it there? What is behind it?..." At the end of the second day, as I was lying all alone, I saw clearly a being, with a part of the head cut off, in a military uniform (or the remains of a military uniform) approaching me and suddenly flinging himself upon my chest, with that half a head, to suck my force. I took a good look, then realised that I was about to die. He was drawing all my life out (for I must tell you that people were dying of pneumonia in three days). I was completely nailed to the bed, without movement, in a deep trance. I could no longer stir and he was pulling. I thought, "This is the end." Then I called on my occult power, I put up a big fight and managed to turn him away so that he could not stay there. And I woke up.

But I had seen. And I had learned, I had understood that the illness originated from beings who had been thrown out of their bodies. I had seen this during the First World War, towards its end, when people were living in trenches and were killed by bombardment. They were in perfectly good health, perfectly fine, and in a second they were thrown out of their bodies, not aware that they were dead. They did not know they no longer had a body and they tried to find in others the life they could not find in themselves. That is, they were turned into countless vampires. And they vampirised upon people. And then, besides that, there was a decomposition of the vital forces of those who fell ill and died. One lived in a kind of thick, sticky cloud made up of all that. And so those who took in this cloud fell ill and usually recovered, but those who were attacked by a being of that kind invariably died, they could not resist. I know how much knowledge and power it took for me to resist. It was irresistible. That is, if they were attacked by a being who was a centre of this whirl of bad forces, they died. And there must have been many of these, a great number. I saw all that and I understood.

When someone came to see me, I asked to be left alone. I lay quietly in my bed and I spent two or three days being absolutely quiet, in concentration, with my consciousness. After that, a friend of ours (a Japanese, a very good friend) came and said to me: "Ah! you were ill? So what I thought was true.... Just imagine, for the last two or three days, there hasn't been a single new case of illness in the town, and most of the people who were ill have been cured, and the number of deaths has become almost negligible, and now it is all over. The disease is totally under control." Then I narrated what had happened to me and he went and told it to everybody. They even published articles about it in the papers.

Well, you see, consciousness is more effective than packets of medicine!... The situation was critical. Just imagine, there were entire villages where everyone had died. There was a village in Japan, not very big, but still with more than a hundred people, and it happened, due to an unusual chance, that one of the villagers was to receive a letter (the postman went there only if there was a letter; naturally, it was a village far out in the country). So he went into the countryside; there was snow; the whole village was under snow... and there was not a living person. It was like that. It was that kind of epidemic. And Tokyo was also like that; but Tokyo was a big city and things did not happen in the same way. And this is how the epidemic ended. That is my story.

Restoring the Equilibrium

Now this brings us naturally to the cure. All that is very well, we now have the knowledge; so, how to prevent illnesses from coming, first of all, and when the illness does occur, how to cure it?

One may try ordinary means and sometimes that succeeds.

It is usually when the body is convinced that it has been given conditions under which it should be well; it resolves to be well and it is cured. But if your body has not the will, the resolution to recover, you may try whatever you like, it won't be cured. This also I know by experience. For I have known people who could be cured in five minutes, even of something considered to be very serious, and I have known people who had an illness that was not fatal, but who cherished it with such persistence that it became fatal. It was impossible to persuade their body to let go of the illness.

And it is here that one must be very careful and look at oneself with great discrimination to discover the small part in oneself that — how to put it? — takes pleasure in being ill. Oh! there are many reasons. There are people who are ill out of spite, there are people who are ill out of hate, there are people who are ill out of despair, there are people... And these movements are nothing formidable. It is quite a small movement in the being; one is vexed and says: "You will see what is going to happen, you will see the consequences of what he has done to me! Let it come! I am going to be ill." One does not say it openly to oneself, for one would scold oneself, but there is something somewhere that thinks in that way.

So there are two things you have to do when you have discovered the disorder, the disharmony, big or small. First, we said that this disharmony creates a kind of tremor and a lack of peace in the physical being, in the body. It is a kind of fever. Even if the fever is not general, there are small localised fevers; there are people who get restless. So the first thing to do is to calm oneself, bring peace, quiet, relaxation, with a total confidence, into this little corner (not necessarily into the whole body). Afterwards you see what is the cause of the disorder. You look. There are many, but still you try to find out approximately the cause of this disorder, and through the pressure of light and knowledge and spiritual force you re-establish the harmony, the proper functioning. And if the ailing part is receptive, if it does not offer any obstinate resistance, you can be cured in a few seconds.

This is not always the case. Sometimes there is, as I have said, a bad will: you are more or less on strike, at least you want the illness to have its consequences. So, that takes a little more time. However, if you do not happen to be of particularly bad will, after some time the Force acts: after a few minutes or hours or at the most some days you are cured.

Now, in the special case of attacks of adverse forces, it gets more complicated, because you have to deal not only with the will of the body (note that I do not accept the argument of those who tell me, "But I do not want to be ill!", for your consciousness always says it does not want to be ill, you would have to be half crazy to say, "I want to be ill"; but it is not your consciousness that wants to be ill, it is some part of your body or, at the most, a fragment of the vital that has gone astray and wishes to be ill, and unless you observe with a good deal of attention you do not notice it). But I say that the situation gets complicated if behind this there is an attack, a pressure from adverse forces who really want to harm you. You may have opened the door through a spiritual error, through a movement of vanity, of anger, of hatred or of violence; even if it is merely a movement that comes and goes, that can open the door. There are always germs watching and only waiting for an occasion. That is why you have to be very careful. Anyway, for some reason or other, the influence has pierced through the shell of protection and acts there encouraging the illness to become as bad as it can be. Then the first method is not quite enough. In that case you have to add something; you must add the Force of spiritual purification which is such an absolutely, perfectly constructive force that nothing that is in the least destructive can survive in it. If you have this Force at your disposal or if you can ask for it and get it, you direct it on the spot and the adverse force usually runs away immediately, because if it happens to be in the midst of this Force it is dissolved, it disappears; for no force of disintegration can survive within this Force. Therefore the disorder disappears and the adverse force disappears with it. It can be changed into a constructive force, that is possible, or it may be simply dissolved and reduced to nothing. And with that not only is the illness cured, but all possibility of its return is also eliminated. You are cured of the disease once for all, it never comes back.[7]

2

Weakness of the Nervous Envelope

The Mother: To whatever cause an illness may be due, material or mental, external or internal, it must, before it can affect the physical body, touch another layer of the being that surrounds and protects it. This subtler layer is called in different teachings by various names, — the etheric body, the nervous envelope. It is a subtle body and yet almost visible. In density something like the vibrations that you see around a very hot and steaming object, it emanates from the physical body and closely covers it. All communications with the exterior world are made through this medium, and it is this that must be invaded and penetrated first before the body can be affected. If this envelope is absolutely strong and intact, you can go into places infested with the worst of diseases, even plague and cholera, and remain quite immune. It is a perfect protection against all possible attacks of illness, so long as it is whole and entire, thoroughly consistent in its composition, its elements in faultless balance. This body is built up, on the one side, of a material basis, but rather of material conditions than of physical matter, on the other, of the vibrations of our psychological states. Peace and equanimity and confidence, faith in health, undisturbed repose and cheerfulness and bright gladness constitute this element in it and give it strength and substance. It is a very sensitive medium with facile and quick reactions; it readily takes in all kinds of suggestions and these can rapidly change and almost remould its condition. A bad suggestion acts very strongly upon it; a good suggestion operates in the contrary sense with the same force. Depression and discouragement have a very adverse effect; they cut out holes in it, as it were, in its very stuff, render it weak and unresisting and open to hostile attacks an easy passage.[8]

How the Forces of Illness Attack

Sri Aurobindo: Attacks of illness are attacks of the lower nature or of adverse forces taking advantage of some weakness, opening or response in the nature, — like all other things that come and have got to be thrown away, they come from outside. If one can feel them so coming and get the strength and the habit to throw them away before they can enter the body, then one can remain free from illness. Even when the attack seems to rise from within, that means only that it has not been detected before it entered the subconscient; once in the subconscient, the force that brought it rouses it from there sooner or later and it invades the system. When you feel it just after it has entered, it is because though it came direct and not through the subconscient, yet you could not detect it while it was still outside. Very often it arrives like that . . . forcing its way through the subtle vital envelope which is our main armour of defence, but it can be stopped there in the envelope itself before it penetrates the material body. Then one may feel some effect, e.g., feverishness or a tendency to cold, but there is not the full invasion of the malady. If it can be stopped earlier or if the vital envelope of itself resists and remains strong, vigorous and intact, then there is no illness; the attack produces no physical effect and leaves no traces.[9]

If it is a question of forces, how or where do these millions of bacilli and viruses come in? Has each force a definite bacillus as its agent?

What is the difficulty? You are like the scientists who say or used to say there is no such thing as mind or thought independent of the physical brain. Mind and thought are only names for brain quiverings. Or that there is no such thing as vital force because all the movements of life depend upon chemicals, glands and what not. These things and the germs also are only a minor physical instrumentation for something supraphysical.

Or do the forces diminish the general resistance of the body in an occult way and germs according to their individual characteristics try to capture the body?

They first weaken or break through the nervous envelope, the aura. If that is strong and whole, a thousand million germs will not be able to do anything to you. The envelope pierced, they attack the subconscient mind in the body; sometimes also the vital mind or mind proper — prepare the illness by fear or thought of illness. The doctors themselves said that in influenza or cholera in the Far East 90 percent got ill through fear. Nothing to take away the resistance like fear. But still the subconscient is the main thing.

But diseases like cholera, plague etc. are supposed to break out by contamination.

If the contrary Force is strong in the body, one can move in the midst of plague and cholera and never get contaminated. . . .

There is a physical aspect to things and there is an occult supraphysical aspect — one need not get in the way of the other. All physical things are the expression of the supraphysical. The existence of a body with physical instruments and processes does not, as the 19th century vainly imagined, disprove the existence of a soul which uses the body even if it is also conditioned by it. Laws of Nature do not disprove the existence of God. The fact of a material world to which our instruments are accorded does not disprove the existence of less material worlds which certain subtler instruments can show to us.[10]

Sensing and Repelling Attacks of Illness

Sri Aurobindo: If we live only in the outward physical consciousness, we do not usually know that we are going to be ill
until the symptoms of the malady declare themselves in the
body. But if we develop the inward physical consciousness,
we become aware of a subtle environmental physical atmosphere and can feel the forces of illness coming towards us
through it, feel them even at a distance and, if we have learned
how to do it, we can stop them by the will or otherwise. We
sense too around us a vital physical or nervous envelope which
radiates from the body and protects it, and we can feel the
adverse forces trying to break through it and can interfere,
stop them or reinforce the nervous envelope. Or we can feel
the symptoms of illness, fever or cold, for instance, in the subtle physical sheath before they are manifest in the gross body
and destroy them there, preventing them from manifesting in
the body.[11]

All illnesses pass through the nervous or vital-physical sheath
of the subtle consciousness and subtle body before they enter
the physical. If one is conscious of the subtle body or with the
subtle consciousness, one can stop an illness on its way and
prevent it from entering the physical body. But it may have
come without one's noticing, or when one is asleep or through
the subconscient, or in a sudden rush when one is off one's
guard; then there is nothing to do but to fight it out from a
hold already gained on the body. Self-defence by these inner
means may become so strong that the body becomes practically immune as many yogis are. Still this "practically" does
not mean "absolutely". The absolute immunity can only come
with the supramental change. For below the supramental it is
the result of an action of a Force among many forces and can
be disturbed by a disruption of the equilibrium established —
in the supramental it is a law of the nature; in the supra-

mentalised body immunity from illness would be automatic, inherent in its new nature.[12]

When Sri Aurobindo says that illness comes from outside, what exactly is it that comes?

The Mother: It is a kind of vibration made up of a mental suggestion, a vital force of disorder and certain physical elements which are the materialisation of the mental suggestion and the vital vibration. And these physical elements can be what they have agreed to call germs, microbes, this and that and many other things.

It may be accompanied by a sensation, it may be accompanied by a taste, it may be accompanied also by a smell, if one has very developed subtle senses. There are these formations of illness which give a special taste to the air, a special smell or a special little sensation.

People have many senses which are asleep. They are terribly tamasic. If all the senses they possess were awake, there are many things they would perceive, which can just pass by without their suspecting anything.

For example, many people have a certain kind of influenza at the moment. It is very widespread. Well, when it comes close, it has a special taste, a special smell, and it brings you a certain contact (naturally not like a blow, something a little more subtle), a certain contact, exactly like when you pass your hand over something, backwards over some material.... You have never done that? The material has a grain, you know; when you pass your hand in the right direction or when you pass it like this (*gesture*), well, it makes you... it is something that passes over your skin, like this, backwards. But naturally, I can tell you, it doesn't come like a staggering blow. It is very subtle but very clear. . . .

There is always a way of isolating oneself by an atmosphere of protection, if one knows how to have an extremely quiet vibration, so quiet that it makes almost a kind of wall around you. But all the time, all the time one is vibrating in response to vibrations which come from outside. If you become aware of that, all the time there is something which does this, this, this, this (*gestures*), which responds to all the vibrations coming from outside. You are never in an absolutely quiet atmosphere which emanates from you, that is, which comes from inside outwards — not something that comes from outside inwards — something which is like an envelope around you, very quiet, like this, and you can go anywhere at all and these vibrations which come from outside do not begin to do this (*gesture*) around your atmosphere.

If you could see that kind of dance, the dance of vibrations which is there around you all the time, you would see, you would understand very well what I mean. . . .

What is to be wondered at is the unconsciousness with which human beings go through life; they don't know how to live, there is not one in a million who knows how to live, and they live like that, somehow or other, limping along, managing, not managing. . . . All the same, one should learn how to live. That is the first thing one ought to teach children: to learn how to live.[13]

Illnesses enter through the subtle body, don't they? How can they be stopped?

If one is very sensitive, very sensitive — one must be very sensitive — the moment they touch the subtle body and try to pass through, one feels it. It is not like something touching the body, it is a sort of impression. If you are able to perceive it at that moment, you have still the power to say "no", and it goes away. But for this one must be extremely sensitive. However, that develops. All these things can be developed methodically by the will. You can become quite conscious of this envelope, and if you develop it enough, you don't even need to look and see, you feel that something has touched you. . . .

One can very easily feel a kind of slight uneasiness (it is not something which is imposed with a great force), a slight uneasiness approaching you from somewhere: in front, behind, above, below. If at that moment you are alert enough, you say "no", as though you were cutting off the contact with great force, and it is finished. If you are not conscious at that moment, the next minute or a few minutes later you get a queer sick feeling inside, a chill in the back, a little discomfort, the beginning of some disharmony; you feel a disharmony somewhere, as though the general harmony had been disturbed. Then you must concentrate all the more and with a great strength of will keep the faith that nothing can do you harm, nothing can touch you. This is enough, you can throw off the illness at that moment. But you must do this immediately, you understand, you must not wait five minutes, it must be done at once. If you wait too long and begin to feel a real uneasiness somewhere, if something begins to get really disturbed, then it is good to sit down, concentrate and call the Force, concentrate it on the place which is getting disturbed, that is to say, which is beginning to become ill. But if you don't do anything at all, an illness really gets lodged somewhere; and all this, because you were not alert enough. And sometimes one has to follow the entire curve to find the favourable moment again and get rid of the thing. I have said somewhere that in the physical domain all is a question of method — a method is necessary for realising everything. And if the illness has succeeded in touching the physical-physical, well, you must follow the procedure needed to get rid of it. This is what medical science calls "the course of the illness". One can hasten the course with the help of spiritual forces, but all the same the procedure must be followed. There are some four different stages. The very first is instantaneous. The second can be done in a few minutes, the third may take several hours and the fourth several days. And then, once the thing is lodged there, all will depend not only on the receptivity of the body but still more on the willingness of the part which is the cause of the disorder. You see, when something comes from outside, it is in affinity with something inside. If it manages to pass through, to enter without one's being aware of it, it means there is an affinity somewhere, and it is this part of the being which has responded that must be convinced.[14]

Psychological States and the Nervous Envelope

The Mother: The vital body surrounds the physical body with a kind of envelope which has almost the same density as the vibrations of heat which one can observe on a very hot day. . . . It is this which protects the body from all contagion, fatigue, exhaustion and even from accidents. So if this envelope is completely intact, it protects you from everything, but a little too strong an emotion, a little fatigue, some dissatisfaction or a shock of any kind is enough to scratch it, as it were, and the slightest scratch allows any sort of intrusion. Medical science also now recognises that if you are in perfect vital equilibrium, you do not catch illnesses or in any case you have a kind of immunity from contagion. If you have this equilibrium, this inner harmony which keeps the envelope intact, it protects you from everything. There are people who lead a perfectly ordinary life, who know how to sleep as they should, eat as they should, and their nervous envelope is so intact that they pass through all dangers as though nothing concerned them. It is a capacity one can cultivate in oneself. If you become aware of the weak spot in your envelope, a few minutes of concentration, of calling to the force, of inner peace are sometimes enough for it to be set right, cured, and for the untoward thing to vanish.[15]

What are the causes of accidents? Are they due to a disequilibrium?

If one answers in depth... Outwardly there are many causes,

but there is a deeper cause which is always there. I said the other day that if the nervous envelope is intact, accidents can be avoided, and even if you have an accident it won't have any consequences. As soon as there is a scratch or a defect in the nervous envelope of the being and according to the nature of this scratch, so to speak, its place, its character, there will be an accident corresponding to the diminution of resistance in the envelope. I believe almost everybody is psychologically aware of one thing: that accidents occur when one has a sort of uncomfortable feeling, when one is not fully conscious and in possession of oneself, when one feels uneasy. In any case, people generally have the impression that they are not fully themselves, not fully aware of what they are doing. If one were fully conscious, the consciousness wide awake, accidents would not occur; one would make just the right gesture, the necessary movement to avoid the accident. Therefore, as an almost absolute rule, it is a slackening of consciousness. . . .

If for some reason or other — for example, lack of sleep, lack of rest, an absorbing preoccupation or all sorts of things that tire you, that is to say, when you are not above them — if the vital envelope is a little damaged, it does not function perfectly and any current of force which passes through is enough to produce an accident. In the final analysis, the accident always comes from that, it is what one may call inattentiveness or a slackening of consciousness. There are days when you feel quite... not exactly uneasy, but as if you were trying to catch something which escapes you, you can't hold yourself together, you are as though half-diluted; these are the days of accidents. You must be careful. Naturally, this is not to tell you to shut yourself up in your room and not move when you feel like that! That is not what I mean. But I mean that you must watch all the more attentively, be all the more on your guard, not allow, precisely, this inattentiveness, this slackening of consciousness to occur.[16]

3

Wrong Thinking

Sri Aurobindo: The feeling of illness is at first only a suggestion; it becomes a reality because your physical consciousness accepts it. It is like a wrong suggestion in the mind, — if the mind accepts it, it becomes clouded and confused and has to struggle back into harmony and clearness. It is so with the body consciousness and illness. You must not accept but reject it with your physical mind and so help the body consciousness to throw off the suggestion. If necessary, make a counter-suggestion "No, I shall be well; I am and shall be all right."[17]

The Mother: The most important thing for good health is control over the mind, because the body obeys almost totally what you *believe*. When you believe that you are ill, you become more and more ill. If you believe that this or that will cure you, there is much chance that it will do so. Right thinking is most necessary for good health.[18]

The mind . . . is the master of the physical being. . . . Only one doesn't know how to use one's mind, quite the contrary. Not only does one not know how to use it, but one uses it as badly as possible. The mind has a considerable power of formation and a direct action on the body, and usually one uses this power to make oneself ill. For as soon as the least thing goes wrong, the mind begins to shape and build all possible catastrophes, to ask itself whether it could be this, whether it could be that, if that is the way it is going to be, and how it will all end.

Well, if instead of letting the mind do this disastrous work, one used the same capacity to make favourable formations — simply, for example, to give confidence to the body, to tell it that it is just a passing disturbance and that it is nothing, and that if it enters a real state of receptivity, the ailment can go away as easily as it came, and that one can cure oneself in a few seconds — if one knows how to do that, one gets wonderful results.[19]

If you live normally, under quite normal conditions — without having extravagant ideas and a depressing education — well, through all your youth and usually till you are about thirty, you have an absolute trust in life. If, for example, you are not surrounded by people who, as soon as you have a cold in the head, get into a flurry and rush to the doctor and give you medicines, if you are in normal surroundings and happen to have something — an accident or a slight illness — there is this certainty in the body, this absolute trust that it will be all right: "It is nothing, it will pass off. It is sure to go. I will be quite well tomorrow or in a few days. It is sure to get better" — whatever you may have caught. That is indeed the normal condition of the body. An absolute trust that all life lies before it and that all will be well. And this helps enormously. One gets cured nine times out of ten, one gets cured very quickly with this confidence: "It is nothing; what is it after all? Just an accident, it will pass off, it is nothing." And there are people who keep this for a very long time, a very long time, a kind of confidence — nothing can happen to them. Their whole life is before them and nothing can happen to them. And what happens to them is of no importance whatsoever: all will surely go well; they have the whole of life before them. Naturally, if you live in surroundings where there are morbid ideas and people spend their time telling you disastrous and catastrophic things, then you may think wrongly. And if you think wrongly, this reacts on your body. . . .

I have seen such cases, children who had these little accidents one has when running about and playing: they did not
even think about it and it went away at once. I have seen others whose families had drummed into them, as soon as they
were old enough to understand, that everything is dangerous,
that there are microbes everywhere, that you must be very
careful, that the least wound may prove disastrous, that you
must be absolutely on your guard so that nothing serious happens.... So they must have their wounds dressed, must be
washed with disinfectants, and there they sit wondering, "What
is going to happen to me? Oh! What if I get tetanus, a septic
fever?..." Naturally, in such cases one loses confidence in life
and the body feels the effects keenly. Three-fourths of its resistance disappears. But normally, naturally, the body knows
it should be healthy and it knows it has the ability to react.
And if something happens, it tells this something: "It is nothing, it will go away, don't think about it, it is over", and it
goes away.[20]

The Power of Thought

The Mother: The power of thought over the body is tremendous! You cannot imagine how tremendous it is. Even a
thought that is subconscious, and sometimes quite unconscious,
acts and produces fantastic results. . . .

Tiny, tiny mental or vital reactions — so small that to our
ordinary consciousness they seem not to have the *least* importance — act upon the body's cells and can create disorders...
When you observe attentively, you suddenly become aware of
a slight uneasiness, a mere nothing (if you are busy, you don't
even notice it), and then if you pursue this uneasiness to see
what it is, you perceive that it comes from something quite
imperceptible and "insignificant" to our active consciousness
— but it is enough to make the body feel uneasy.

That is why, unless you can be at will and constantly in
what they call here the Brahmic consciousness, it is practi-

cally impossible to control. And this is what gives the impression that certain things happen in the body independently of... not only of our will but of our consciousness — *it is not true.*

Only there is everything that comes from outside — that is what is most dangerous. Constantly, constantly — you eat, you catch it... what a mass of vibrations! The vibrations of the thing you are eating, when it was alive (they always remain), the vibrations of the person who cooked it, the vibrations of... All the time, all the time, it never stops — you breathe, it enters. Naturally when you start talking to someone or mixing with people, then you become a little more conscious of what is coming, but even when you are just sitting still, not paying attention to others, it comes. There is an almost total interdependence — isolation is an illusion. By reinforcing your atmosphere (*Mother gestures, as if building a wall around herself*), you can keep these things at a distance *to a certain extent.* ...

But I know absolutely that once this whole mass of the physical mind is mastered and the Brahmic consciousness is brought into it in a continuous way, you *can...* you become the *master* of your health.

And that is why I tell people (not that I expect them to be able to do it, at least not now, but it is good to know it) that it is *not* a matter of fate, that it is *not* something that completely escapes our control, that it is *not* some sort of "law of Nature" over which we have no power — it is not so. We are truly the masters of everything that has been brought together to create our transitory individuality; and the power of control is given to us, if we know how to use it.[21]

My own experience is going on in the minutest details. These details are imperceptible in themselves but point in a certain direction which, more and more, is this: when you take a wrong attitude, it immediately sets off every disorder. It is almost as if you shifted into the wrong gear — that is not it, because "gear" is too rigid — but let us say the whole universe is rolling along smoothly, and it is only when you go like this or like that (*Mother indicates changes of position like a sort of shifting of gears*) that disorders appear. There are many ways to have a wrong attitude. It is as if you shifted gears a little: things still work (assuming the mechanism to be particularly supple) but they grate — they grate and therefore wear out and deteriorate and break down. But if they were in the right position, there would be no friction.

It is the sense of friction which no longer exists — it disappears, there is no friction. The friction results only from the wrong angle, from something like a shift of position.

Of course, this is much easier to express in psychological terms — psychologically, it is very simple, crystal clear — but even *materially* it is like that.[22]

The Mentality of the Cells

The Mother: [*To someone with a cyst:*] You know, the trick (there is a trick) is to tell the cells that this is not at all what is expected of them . . . that what is expected of them is not to gather into a bundle there, like that; it isn't their duty to do that — you must convince them.

It is rather odd. It is the origin of habits; they have the impression: "This is what we have to do, this is what we have to do, this is what..." (*Mother turns a finger in a circle*).

It is the same thing with me, but I have told them. Only, you have to be conscious of the movement, and then very quietly but very, very confidently, very confidently, tell them as you would children, "No, it isn't your duty to do that; that isn't your duty."

All chronic illnesses come from this. There may be an accident (something happens, an accident) and then there is a sort of submissive and unconscious goodwill that causes it [the result of the accident] to be repeated: "We must repeat it, we must repeat it, we must repeat it..." (*circular gesture*). And it stops only if there is a consciousness in contact with them which can make them understand: "No, in this case, you must not go on repeating!" (*Mother laughs*)

There are cases where this power of repetition is extremely useful. I even think it is what gives stability to the form, otherwise we would change form or appearance, or we would liquefy. It is what works for durability.

There is this habit of repetition, and then the feeling of fatality. For example, if you receive a blow or something is wrong with you, at once there is this sense of fatality: "Ah, now it is like that, now it is like that..." (*same circular gesture*). So here also (all this is going on in the consciousness of the cells), here also you must tell them: "No! It is not irreparable: if you do this" (for instance, something has been accidentally twisted), "if you make a movement in the other direction, it can be set right."

It is not at all by brilliant displays of will and powers, that isn't it: it is a very, very quiet power of persuasion — exerted very gently but very confidently and very persistently. None of the vital things work — they have a momentary effect, then it is over.

Oh, it is very interesting. But one has to be very modest to do this work, one cannot be fond of brilliant displays — very modest. And very quiet.[23]

4

Fear

The Mother: Ninety percent of illnesses are the result of the subconscient fear of the body. In the ordinary consciousness of the body there is a more or less hidden anxiety about the consequences of the slightest physical disturbance. It can be translated by these words of doubt about the future: "And what will happen?" It is this anxiety that must be checked. Indeed this anxiety is a lack of confidence in the Divine's Grace, the unmistakable sign that the consecration is not complete and perfect.

As a practical means of overcoming this subconscient fear each time that something of it comes to the surface, the more enlightened part of the being must impress on the body the necessity of an entire trust in the Divine's Grace, the certitude that this Grace is always working for the best in our self as well as in all, and the determination to submit entirely and unreservedly to the Divine's Will.

The body must know and be convinced that its essence is divine and that if no obstacle is put in the way of the Divine's working nothing can harm us. This process must be steadily repeated until all recurrence of fear is stopped. And then even if the illness succeeds in making its appearance, its strength and duration will be considerably diminished until it is definitively conquered.[24]

Do not torment yourself and do not worry; above all try to banish all fear; fear is a dangerous thing which can give importance to something which had none at all. The mere fear of seeing certain symptoms renew themselves is enough to bring about this repetition.[25]

Fear is hidden consent. When you are afraid of something, it means that you admit its possibility and thus strengthen its hand. It can be said that it is a subconscient consent.[26]

Sweet Mother, when one sees an illness coming, how can one stop it?

Ah! First of all, you must not want it, and nothing in the body must want it. You must have a very strong will not to be ill. This is the first condition.

The second condition is to call the light, a light of equilibrium, a light of peace, quietude and balance, and to push it into all the cells of the body, enjoining them not to be afraid, because that is the second condition.

First, not to want to be ill, and then not to be afraid of illness. You must neither attract it nor tremble. You must not want illness at all. But it must not be because of fear that you do not want it; you must not be afraid. You must have a calm certitude and a complete trust in the power of the Grace to shelter you from everything, and then think of something else, not be concerned about it any longer. When you have done these two things, refusing the illness with all your will and infusing a confidence which completely eliminates fear in the cells of the body, and then occupied yourself with something else, not thinking any more about the illness, forgetting that it exists... if you know how to do that, you may even be in contact with people who have contagious diseases, and yet you do not catch them. But you must know how to do it.

Many people say, "Oh, no, I am not afraid." They have no fear in the mind, their mind is not afraid, it is strong, it has no fear; but the body trembles and they don't know it, because it is in the cells of the body that the trembling goes on. It trembles with a terrible anxiety and this is what attracts the illness. It is there that you must put the Force, and the quietude of a perfect peace and an absolute trust in the Grace. And then sometimes you have to drive away with a similar force in your thought all suggestions that, after all, the physical world is full of illnesses and these are contagious, and because you were in contact with someone who is ill, you are sure to catch it, and then that inner methods are not powerful enough to act on the physical, and all kinds of stupidities which the air is full of. These are collective suggestions everyone passes from one to another.[27]

Fear and Contagion

The Mother: When one is in a normal state of equilibrium and lives in a normal physical harmony, the body has a capacity of resistance, it has within it an atmosphere strong enough to resist illnesses: its most material substance emanates subtle vibrations which have the strength to resist illnesses, even diseases which are called contagious — in fact, all vibrations are contagious, but still, certain diseases are considered especially contagious. Well, a man who, even from the purely external point of view, is in a state of harmony in the functioning of his organs and an adequate psychological balance, has at the same time enough resistance for the contagion not to affect him. But if for some reason or other he loses this equilibrium or is weakened by depression, dissatisfaction, psychological difficulties or undue fatigue, for instance, this reduces the normal resistance of the body and he is open to the disease. . . .

From the ordinary point of view, in most cases, it is usually fear — fear, which may be mental fear, vital fear, but which is almost always physical fear, a fear in the cells — it is fear which opens the door to all contagion. Mental fear — all who have a little control over themselves or any human dignity can eliminate it. Vital fear is more subtle and asks for a greater control.

As for physical fear, a veritable yoga is necessary to overcome it, for the cells of the body are afraid of everything that is unpleasant or painful, and as soon as there is any discomfort, even if it is insignificant, the cells of the body become anxious; they don't like to be uncomfortable. And then, to overcome that, the control of a conscious will is necessary. It is usually this kind of fear that opens the door to illnesses. And I am not speaking of the first two types of fear which, as I said, any human being who wants to be human in the noblest sense of the word must overcome, for that is cowardice. But physical fear is more difficult to overcome; without it even the most violent attacks could be repelled. If one has a minimum of control over the body, one can lessen its effects, but that is not immunity. It is this kind of trembling of material, physical fear in the cells of the body which aggravates all illnesses.

Some people are spontaneously free from fear even in their body; they have enough vital equilibrium in them not to be afraid, not to fear, and a natural harmony in the rhythm of their physical life which enables them to reduce the illness spontaneously to a minimum. There are others, on the other hand, with whom it always becomes as bad as it can be, some-times to the point of catastrophe. There is the whole range and this can be seen very easily. Well, this depends on a kind of happy rhythm of the movement of life in them which is harmonious enough to resist attacks of illness from outside, or else which doesn't exist or is not strong enough and is re-placed by that trembling of fear, that kind of instinctive an-guish which turns the least unpleasant contact into something painful and harmful. There is the whole range, from someone who can go through the worst contagion and epidemics with-out ever catching anything to one who falls ill at the slightest chance. So naturally it always depends on the constitution of each person; and as soon as you want to make an effort to progress, it naturally depends on the control you have acquired over yourself, until the moment when the body becomes the docile instrument of the higher Will and you can obtain from it a normal resistance to all attacks.

But when you can eliminate fear, you are practically safe. For example, epidemics, or so-called epidemics, like those which are raging at present — ninety-nine times out of a hundred they come from fear: a fear, then, which even becomes a mental fear in its most sordid form, promoted by newspaper articles, useless talk and so on.[28]

What is the difference between mental, vital and physical fear?

If you are conscious of the movement of your mind, the movement of your vital and the movement of your physical, you know it.

The mental is very simple: it is thoughts. You start thinking, for example, that there is this illness, and this illness is very contagious, and perhaps you will catch it, and if you catch it, it will be terrible, and what is to be done to keep from catching it?... And so the mind begins to tremble: what will happen tomorrow? etc.

The vital, you feel. You feel it in your sensations. All at once you feel hot, you feel cold, you perspire or all kinds of unpleasant things happen. And then you feel your heart beating fast and suddenly you have fever and then the circulation stops and you become cold.

Physically, well... When you no longer have the other two fears, you can become aware of the physical fear. Generally, the other two are much more conscious. They hide the physical fear from you. But when you no longer have any mental or vital fear, then you notice it. It is a peculiar little vibration that gets into your cells and they begin to shiver like this. But the cells are not like a heart that starts beating very fast. It is in the cells themselves: they tremble, a slight quivering. And it is very difficult to control. Yet it can be controlled.[29]

One thing that is now beginning to be recognised by everyone, even by the medical profession, is that hygienic measures, for example, are effective only to the extent that one has confidence in them. Take the case of an epidemic. Many years ago we had a cholera epidemic here — it was bad — but the chief medical officer at the hospital was a very energetic man and he decided to vaccinate everyone. When he discharged the vaccinated people, he would tell them, "Now you are vaccinated and nothing will happen to you, but if you were not vaccinated you would be sure to die!" He told them this with great authority. Usually such an epidemic lasts a long time and it is difficult to arrest it, but in a fortnight, I think, this doctor succeeded in checking it; in any case, it was done miraculously fast. But he knew very well that the best effect of his vaccination was the confidence it gave to people.

Now, quite recently, they have found something else and I consider it wonderful. They have discovered that for every disease there is a microbe that cures it (call it a microbe if you like, anyway, some sort of germ). But what is so extraordinary is that this "microbe" is extremely contagious, even more contagious than the microbe of the disease. And it generally develops under two conditions: in those who have a sort of natural good humour and energy and in those who have a strong will to get well! Suddenly they catch the "microbe" and are cured. And what is wonderful is that if there is one who is cured in an epidemic, three more recover immediately. And this "microbe" is found in all who are cured.

But I am going to tell you something: what people take to be a microbe is simply the materialisation of a vibration or a will from another world. When I learned of these medical discoveries, I said to myself, "Truly, science is making progress." One might almost say with greater reason, "Matter is progressing", it is becoming more and more receptive to a higher will. And what is translated in their science as "microbes" will be seen, if one goes to the root of things, to be simply a vibratory mode; and this vibratory mode is the material translation of a higher will. If you can bring this force or this will, this power, this vibration (call it what you like) into a given set of circumstances, not only will it act in you but it will act, through contagion, all around you.[30]

Sanitation and Health

But has it not been found that by improved sanitation the health of the average citizen improves?

The Mother: Medicine and sanitation are indispensable in the ordinary life. . . . Still there is this disadvantage of sanitation that while you diminish the chance of catching an illness, you diminish also your natural power of resistance. Attendants in hospitals, who are always washing with disinfectants, find that their hands become more easily infected and are much more susceptible than the hands of others. There are people, on the contrary, who know nothing of hygiene and do the most unsanitary things and yet remain immune. Their very ignorance helps them because it shuts them to the suggestions that come with medical knowledge. On the other hand, your belief in the sanitary precautions you take helps them to work. For your thought is, "Now I am disinfected and safe", and to that extent it makes you safe.

But why then are we to take sanitary precautions such as drinking only filtered water?

Is any one of you pure and strong enough not to be affected by suggestions? If you drink unfiltered water and think, "Now I am drinking impure water", you have every chance of falling sick. And even though such suggestions may not enter through the conscious mind, the whole of your subconscious is there, almost helplessly open to take any kind of suggestion. In life it is the action of the subconscious that has the larger share and it acts a hundred times more powerfully than the conscious parts. The normal human condition is a state filled with apprehensions and fears: if you observe your mind deeply for ten minutes, you will find that for nine out of ten it is full of fears — it carries in it fear about many things, big and small, near and far, seen and unseen, and though you do not usually take conscious notice of it, it is there all the same. To be free from all fear can come only by steady effort and discipline.

And even if by discipline and effort you have liberated your mind and your vital of apprehension and fear, it is more difficult to convince the body. But that too must be done. Once you enter the path of Yoga you must get rid of all fears — the fears of your mind, the fears of your vital, the fears of your body which are lodged in its very cells. One of the uses of the blows and knocks you receive on the path of Yoga is to rid you of all fear. The causes of your fears leap on you again and again, until you can stand before them free and indifferent, untouched and pure. One has a fear of the sea, another the fear of fire. The latter will find, it may be, that he has to face conflagration after conflagration till he is so trained that not a cell of his body quivers. That of which you have horror comes repeatedly till the horror is gone. One who seeks the transformation and is a follower of the Path, must become through and through fearless, not to be touched or shaken by anything whatever in any part of his nature.[31]

Even so, there are microbes in water?

I have seen, here in this country, village people who had nothing to drink but water that was no longer water, it was mere mud. I have seen it with my own eyes. It was yellowish mud in which cows had bathed and done all the rest and people had waded through it after walking on the roads. They threw their rubbish there and everything was in it. And then I saw these people. They entered it; it was yellow mud and there at the end there was a little bit of water — it was not water, it was yellowish, you know — they bent over, collected this water in their palms and drank it. And there were some who did not even let it settle. Some knew what to put in it, the herbs needed to make it settle, and it becomes a little clearer if it is left long enough. But there were some who knew nothing at all and drank it as it was. I found out that there was an epidemic of cholera just then in the surrounding area and I said: "There are people still alive in that village with such water?" I was told: "We do not have a single case of cholera...." They had become immune, they were used to it. But if a single one of them had caught it by chance, probably all would have died; because then fear would have entered, and due to the fear they would have had no more resistance, for they were poor miserable things. . . .

There are sadhus, you know, who accept filthy living conditions out of saintliness. They never wash themselves, they do nothing that hygiene demands. They live in a truly filthy condition — and they are free from all illness. Probably because they have faith and they do it purposely. Their morale is magnificent.... I am speaking of sincere people and not those who pretend. They have faith. They do not think of their body, they think of the life of their soul. They have no illness. There are some who come to a state in which an arm or a leg or some part of the body has become completely stiff due to their ascetic posture. They cannot move any more; anyone else would die under such conditions; they continue to live because they have faith, because they do it purposely, because it is something they have imposed on themselves.

Therefore, the moral condition of people is much more important than the physical. If you were in surroundings where everyone was clean and you went for three days without taking a bath, you would get sick. This is not to say that you should not take baths! Because we do not want to be sadhus, we want to be yogis. It is not the same thing. And we want the body to take part in the yoga. So we must do whatever is necessary to keep it in good shape. However, this is to tell you that the moral condition is much more important than the physical.[32]

Getting Rid of Fear

The Mother: There is a small remedy which is very, very easy. For it is based simply on a little question of personal common sense.... You must make a small observation, tell yourself that when you are afraid, it is as though the fear was attracting the thing you are afraid of. If you are afraid of illness, it is as though you were attracting the illness. If you are afraid of an accident, it is as though you were attracting the accident. And if you look into yourself or around yourself a little, you will realise this; it is a patent fact. So if you have just a little common sense, you say: "It is stupid to be afraid of anything, for it is just as though I were making a sign to that thing to come to me. If I had an enemy who wanted to kill me, I would not go and tell him: 'You know, I am the one you want to kill!'" It is something like that. So since fear is bad, we won't have it. And if you say you are unable to prevent it by your reason, well, that shows you have no control over yourselves and must make a little effort to control yourselves. That is all.

Oh! There are many ways to cure oneself of fear. But in the end, each finds his own way which is good for him. There are people to whom it would be enough to say: "Your fear is a weakness", and they would immediately find a way to look at it with contempt, for they have a horror of weakness. There are others to whom you can say: "Fear is a suggestion from hostile forces, you must drive it away as you drive away hostile forces", and that works very well. For each it is different. But first of all you must know that fear is very bad. It is a very bad thing; it is a solvent, it is like an acid. If you put a drop of it on something, it eats into the substance. The first step is not to admit the possibility of fear. Yes, that is the first step. I have known people who boasted about their fear. These are incurable. That is, they would say quite naturally, "Ah, just imagine, I was so frightened!" And so what! It is nothing to be proud of. With such people you can do nothing.

However, once you recognise that fear is not a good thing, that it is neither beneficial nor noble nor worthy of a somewhat enlightened consciousness, you begin to fight against it. And as I have said, the way that is good for one is not good for another; you must find your own way. It depends on each person. Fear is also something terribly collective and contagious — it is contagious, it can be caught more easily than the most contagious illness. You breathe an atmosphere of fear and instantly you feel frightened, without even knowing why or how, nothing, simply because there was an atmosphere of fear. A panic at an accident is nothing but an atmosphere of fear spreading over everyone. And it is quite curable. There have been numerous cases of a panic being stopped outright simply because some people refused the suggestion and could counteract it with an opposite suggestion.   For mystics the best cure, as soon as one begins to feel afraid of something, is to think of the Divine. Then you nestle in his arms or at his feet and leave him entirely responsible for everything that happens, within, outside, everywhere — and immediately the fear disappears. That is the cure for the mystic. It is the easiest of all. But everybody does not enjoy the grace of being a mystic.[33]

Why is it so difficult to convince the body [to be free from fear], when one has succeeded in liberating oneself mentally and vitally?

Because in the vast majority of cases, the body receives its inspirations from the subconscient, it is under the influence of the subconscient. All the fears driven out from the active consciousness go and take refuge there and then, naturally, they have to be chased out from the subconscient and uprooted from there.

Why does one feel afraid?

I suppose it is because one is egoistic!

There are three reasons. First, an excessive concern about one's security. Next, what one does not know always gives an uneasy feeling which is translated in the consciousness by fear. And above all, because one is not in the habit of having a spontaneous trust in the Divine. If you push things far enough, this is the real reason. There are people who do not even know that That exists, but you could tell them in other words, "You have no faith in your destiny" or "You know nothing about Grace" — anything whatever, you may put it as you like, but the root of the matter is a lack of trust. If one always had the feeling that it is the best that happens in all circumstances, one would not be afraid.

The first movement of fear comes automatically. There was a great scientist who was also a great psychologist (I don't remember his name now); he had developed his inner consciousness but wanted to test it. So he undertook an experiment. He wanted to know if, by consciousness, one could control the reflexes of the body (probably he had not gone far enough to do it, for it can be done; in any case, for him it was still impossible). Well, he went to the zoological garden, to the place where snakes were kept in a glass cage. There was a particularly aggressive cobra there; when it was not asleep, it was almost always in a fury, for through the glass it could see people and that irritated it terribly. Our scientist went and stood in front of the cage. He knew very well that it was made in such a way that the snake could never break the glass and that he ran no risk of being attacked. So from there he began to excite the snake by shouts, gestures, etc. The cobra, furious, hurled itself against the glass, and every time it did so the scientist closed his eyes! Our psychologist told himself, "But look here, I know this snake cannot pass through, so why do I close my eyes?" Well, one has to admit it is hard to overcome. It is a sense of self-protection, and if one feels one cannot protect oneself, one is afraid. But the movement of fear which is expressed by a blinking of the eyes is not a mental or a vital fear: it is a fear in the cells of the body; for it has not been impressed upon them that there is no danger and they do not know how to resist. It is because one has not done yoga, you see. With yoga one can watch with open eyes, one would not close them; but one would not close the eyes because one calls upon something else, and that "something else" is the sense of the divine Presence in oneself which is stronger than everything.

This is the only thing that can cure you of your fear.[34]

The Subconscient

Sri Aurobindo: In our yoga we mean by the subconscient that quite submerged part of our being in which there is no wakingly conscious and coherent thought, will or feeling or organized reaction, but which yet receives obscurely the impressions of all things and stores them up in itself and from it too all sorts of stimuli, of persistent habitual movements, crudely repeated or disguised in strange forms can surge up into dream or into the waking nature. . . . It is largely responsible for our illnesses; chronic or repeated illnesses are indeed mainly due to the subconscient and its obstinate memory and habit of repetition of whatever has impressed itself upon the body-consciousness. But this subconscient must be clearly distinguished from the subliminal parts of our being such as the inner or subtle physical consciousness, the inner vital or inner mental; for these are not at all obscure or incoherent or ill-organized, but only veiled from our surface consciousness. Our surface constantly receives something, inner touches, communications or influences, from these sources but does not know for the most part whence they come.[35]

The subconscient influences the body because all in the body has developed out of the subconscient and all in itself still is only half conscious and much of its action can be called subconscious. It is therefore much more easily influenced by the subconscious than by the conscious mind and conscious will or even the vital mind and vital will except in those things in which a conscious mental or vital control has been established and the subconscious itself has accepted it. If it were not so, man's control of his actions and physical states would be complete, there would be no illness or if there were, it would be immediately cured by mental action. But it is not so. For that reason the higher consciousness has to be brought down, the body and the subconscient enlightened by it and accustomed to obey its control.[36]

Sweet Mother, is the subconscient stronger than the mind, vital and physical?

The Mother: It has more effect. Precisely because it is subconscious, it is everywhere; everything is as if steeped in the subconscient. And then, "subconscient" means half-conscious: not conscious and not unconscious. It is just between the two; it is like this, half-way; so things slide down into it, one doesn't know they are there, and from there they act; and it is because one doesn't know they are there that they can remain there. There are many things one doesn't want to keep and drives out from the active consciousness, but they go down there, hide there, and because it is subconscious one doesn't notice them; but they have not gone completely, and when they have a chance to come up again, they come up. For example, there are bad habits of the body, in the sense that the body is in the habit of getting out of balance — it is called falling ill; but in any case, the functioning becomes faulty due to a bad habit. By concentrating the Force and directing it on this defect you manage to make it disappear, but it doesn't disappear completely; it enters the subconscient. And then, when you are off your guard, when you stop paying close attention to prevent it from manifesting, it rises up and comes out. You thought, perhaps for months or even years, that you were completely rid of a certain kind of illness you suffered from, and you pay it no more attention; then suddenly one day it returns as though it had never gone. It springs up again from the subconscient. And unless you enter into this subconscient and change things there, that is, unless you change the subconscious into the conscious, it always happens like that. The method is to change the subconscious into the conscious — if each thing that rises to the surface becomes conscious, at that moment it must be changed. There is a still more direct method, it is to enter the subconscient with one's full consciousness and work there; but that is difficult. Yet so long as this is not done, all the progress one has made — I mean physically, in one's body — can always be undone.[37]

Recurrent Illnesses and the Subconscient

Mother, there are people who suffer from certain illnesses year after year, don't they? If one observes the illness, one sees that it comes at a particular time of the year, and this is repeated the next year also, and so on. But the time is fixed. Then what is the reason, and how can one get rid of it?

The Mother: There could be many reasons. It depends on the person you ask. If you ask an astrologer, he will tell you: "It is the stars; when the stars come into the same position, the same conditions recur." Well, this is not so far from the truth. It can be like that. It can also be an individual reaction to certain climatic conditions, or to the position of the sun; or it may be quite simply a bad habit, that's all.

And if you form... If by chance it has happened to you twice in succession, then you form... you have a nice formation, you see, which remains like this (*gesture*) in the subconscient, without showing itself — if you don't observe it! And then when the time draws near, very gently it gives you a push from within to tell you: "Take care, the time is coming, the time is coming, the time is coming!" So naturally it happens, too. Usually it is something like that.

But almost everything that happens physically is like that. The first time, it may be simply a combination of circumstances; then the mind intervenes and makes a construction.

Now, if you accept the construction, you can be sure it will act automatically with clockwork precision. But even if you say, "Oh, nonsense, it is only an idea!" and do this (*gesture*), still the idea, instead of going away, enters inside, into the subconscient — just the subconscious part of the mind — and there it remains quietly. And then, when it is time to manifest itself, from within, like this, it gives a kind of... as though it were tickling the memory a little, nothing more than that, just like this. If it scratches the memory just a little, like this, then suddenly one day you remember: "Why, last year at this time I was ill." And crash! That is it, it has entered. It has entered the zone of the active consciousness, and a few days later it happens.

. . . The body remembers for a very long time. If you want to be completely cured, you must cure this memory in the body, it is absolutely indispensable. And whether you know it or not, you work to cure the memory in the body. When the memory is erased, the body is truly healed.

But unfortunately, instead of destroying the memory, one represses it. Most of the time one pushes it down into the subconscient, and sometimes into the inconscient, still deeper. But then, if it is repressed, if it is not completely erased, very gently, very gently, without seeming like anything, it comes back to the surface; and something you have been cured of for years, if by chance it crosses your mind, just like this, like a little arrow, no longer than that, like an arrow passing by: "Why, at this time I had that", you may be sure that sooner or later — a few seconds, a few minutes, a few hours or days later — it will return. You can... It may come back in a much milder form, it may come in the same form, it may come even more strongly. That depends on your inner state. If you are in a pessimistic state, it will come back more strongly. If you are in an optimistic state, it will be much weaker. But it will come back, and you will have to start the battle with your body's memory all over again so as to destroy it — if this time you are more attentive. If you can destroy it, you are cured. But if you don't destroy it, it will return. It will take a longer or shorter time, it will be more or less complete, but it will return. It can come back in a flash. If you are wide awake and, when it comes, have enough knowledge and clear-sightedness to tell yourself, "Look, here is that wretched memory come again to play its tricks", then you can strike it a violent blow and destroy its reality. If you know how to do that, it is a chance to get rid of it once for all. But it is not very easy to do.

How to do it?

... It is a certain dissolving power which can undo formations. It depends on the nature of the formation. If it is, as in this case, a formation of an adverse kind, then you need the force of a perfectly pure constructive light. If you have this at your disposal, all you have to do is to bombard the thing with that, and you can dissolve it. But it is an operation that has to be performed with inner forces; it cannot be done physically.

That is why all physical remedies are simply palliatives; they are not cures, because they are not enough to touch the living centre of the thing.[38]

Removing the Psychological Roots of Illness

Sri Aurobindo: Absolute cure of an illness so that it cannot return again depends on clearing the mind, the vital and the body consciousness and the subconscient of the psychological response to the force bringing the illness. Sometimes this is done by a sort of order from above (when the consciousness is ready, but it cannot always be done like that). The complete immunity from all illness for which our Yoga tries can only come by a total and permanent enlightenment of the below from above resulting in the removal of the psychological roots of ill health — it cannot be done otherwise.[39]

Can one learn to control one's subconscient as one controls one's conscious thought?

The Mother: It is especially during the body's sleep that one is in contact with the subconscient. In becoming conscious of one's nights, control of the subconscient becomes much easier.

The control can become total when the cells become conscious of the Divine in them and when they open themselves voluntarily to His influence. This is what the consciousness that descended on the earth last year [1969] is working for. Little by little the subconscient automatism of the body is being replaced by the consciousness of the Divine Presence governing the entire functioning of the body.[40]

Part Two

Cure by Inner Means

The difficulties that come to you are exactly in proportion to your strength — nothing can happen to you that does not belong to your consciousness, and all that belongs to your consciousness you are able to master.[1]

The Mother

1

Use of the Will

Sri Aurobindo: Certainly, one can act from within on an illness and cure it. Only it is not always easy as there is much resistance in Matter, a resistance of inertia. An untiring persistence is necessary; at first one may fail altogether or the symptoms increase, but gradually the control of the body or of a particular illness becomes stronger. Again, to cure an occasional attack of illness by inner means is comparatively easy, to make the body immune from it in future is more difficult. A chronic malady is harder to deal with, more reluctant to disappear entirely than an occasional disturbance of the body. So long as the control of the body is imperfect, there are all these and other imperfections and difficulties in the use of the inner force.

If you can succeed by the inner action in preventing increase, even that is something; you have then by *abhyāsa* [practice] to strengthen the power till it becomes able to cure. Note that so long as the power is not entirely there, some aid of physical means need not be altogether rejected.[2]

Above all, do not harbour that idea of an unfit body. . . . Appearances and facts may be all in its favour, but the first condition of success for the yogin and indeed for anybody who wants to do anything great or unusual is to be superior to facts and disbelieve in appearances. Will to be free from disease, however formidable, many-faced or constant its attacks, and repel all contrary suggestions.[3]

What should be the Sadhak's attitude with regard to physical illness?

He must first of all remain completely detached in the vital being and in the mind. The illness is the result of the working of the forces of Nature. He must use his will to reject the illness and one's will must be used as a representative of the Divine Will. When the Divine Will descends into the Adhara then it works no longer indirectly through the Sadhak's will but directly and removes the illness.[4]

Action of the Will on the Body and the Subconscient

Sri Aurobindo: By will to illness I meant this that there is something in the body that accepts the illness and has certain reactions that make this acceptance effective — so there must always be a contrary will in the conscious parts of the being to get rid of this most physical acceptance.[5]

How to put a will even in the subconscient?

Just as you put a will anywhere else — in the vital, in the physical — it has only to be imposed on the consciousness and addressed through the consciousness to the subconscient part of the being.[6]

You must put a conscious will before going to sleep. . . .   A suggestion of that kind on the subconscient is often successful, if not at once, after a time; for the subconscient learns to obey the will put upon it in the waking state.[7]

The Mother: Wake up in yourself a will to conquer. Not a mere will in the mind but a will in the very cells of your body. Without that you can't do anything; you may take a hundred medicines but they won't cure you.[8]

If you remain truly still (it is difficult to be really and truly still — in the vital and the mind it is very easy, but in the body's cells, to be perfectly still *without being tamasic* is a little difficult, it has to be learned), but when you are able to be truly still, there is *always* a little light — a warm little light, very bright and wonderfully still, behind; as if it were saying, "You only have to will." Then the body's cells panic: "Will, how? How can I? The illness is on me, I am overcome. How can I? It is *an illness*" — the whole drama. . . . Then something with a general wisdom says, "Calm down, calm down, (*laughing*) don't be attached to your illness! Calm down. As if you wanted to be ill! Calm down." So they consent — "consent", you know, like a child who has been scolded, "All right, very well, I'll try." They try — immediately, again, that little light comes: "You only have to will."[9]

Cultivating the Will

Sri Aurobindo: Will is not mental effort, it is not the vital push which men use in general to satisfy their desires. It is not strong wishing either; will is not a struggling, striving and unquiet thing. It is calm. When it is calm it is really a call for the Higher Power to come down and act. There is a will which works by dominating over Nature. Another kind of will does not so much dominate as aspires in a prayerful mood for the Higher Power to come down. The highest will is the Divine Will. It is that which is indispensable to all success, it acts automatically.[10]

You have not to be troubled, shaken or restless, but you have not to accept illness as the Divine Will, but rather look upon it as an imperfection of the body to be got rid of as you try to get rid of vital imperfections or mental errors.[11]

The Mother: You must put a strong will for getting rid of your illness and you must remain quiet and unperturbed by the results. The two are not contradictory. One should accompany the other.[12]

The will can be cultivated and developed just as the muscles can, by methodical and progressive exercise. You must not shrink from demanding the maximum effort of your will even for a thing that seems of no importance, for it is through effort that its capacity grows, gradually acquiring the power to apply itself even to the most difficult things. What you have decided to do, you must do, whatever the cost, even if you have to renew your effort over and over again any number of times in order to do it. Your will will be strengthened by the effort and you will have only to choose with discernment the goal to which you will apply it.[13]

The Power of Sincerity

The Mother: You say, "I want to be cured of this"; unfortunately it is not enough to say "I want", there are other parts of the consciousness which hide themselves so that you may not take any notice of them, and when your attention is turned away these parts try to assert themselves. That is why I say and shall always repeat: Be perfectly sincere; do not try to deceive yourself, do not say, "I have done all I can." If you do not succeed, it means that you are not doing all you can. For if you truly do "all" that you can, you will surely succeed. . . .

Even the things and suggestions that come from outside can touch you only in proportion to the consent of your consciousness, and you are made to be the master of your consciousness. If you say, "I have done all I can and it continues in spite of everything, so I give up", you may be sure in advance that you have not done what you could. When an error persists "in spite of everything", it means that something hidden in your being springs up suddenly like a Jack-in-the-box and takes the helm of your life. Hence, there is only one thing to do: it is to go hunting for all the little dark corners which lie hidden in you, and if you put just a tiny spark of goodwill on this darkness, it will yield, it will vanish, and what seemed impossible to you will become not only possible, practicable, but *it will be done*. In this way you can in one minute get rid of a difficulty that would have harassed you for years. I absolutely assure you of it. It depends only on one thing: that you truly, sincerely, want to get rid of it. And it is the same for everything, from physical illnesses up to the highest mental difficulties.[14]

2

Imagination and Faith

The Mother: Imagination is a power of formation. In fact, people who have no imagination are not formative from the mental point of view, they cannot give a concrete power to their thought. Imagination is a very powerful means of action. For instance, if you have a pain somewhere and if you imagine that you are making the pain disappear or are removing it or destroying it — all kinds of images like that — you can perfectly well succeed.[15]

Sweet Mother, what does "a Couéistic optimism" mean?

Ah! Coué. You don't know the story of Coué? Coué was a doctor. He healed people with a psychological treatment, auto-suggestion, which he called the true working of the imagination; and what he defined as imagination was faith. And so he treated all his patients in this way: they had to make a kind of imaginative formation which consisted in thinking themselves cured or in any case recovering, and to repeat this formation to themselves with enough persistence for it to have an effect. He had very remarkable results. He cured lots of people; only, he failed also, and perhaps these were not very lasting cures, I don't know about that. But in any case, this made many people reflect on something that is quite true and of capital importance: that the mind is a formative instrument and that if one knows how to use it in the right way, one gets a good result. He observed — and I think it is true, my observation agrees with his — that people spend their time thinking wrongly. Their mental activity is almost always half pessimistic, and even half destructive. They are all the time thinking of and foreseeing bad things which may happen, untoward consequences of what they have done, and they construct all kinds of catastrophes with an exuberant imagination which, if it were utilised in the other way, would naturally have opposite and more satisfactory results.

If you observe yourself, if you... how to put it?... if you catch yourself thinking — well, if you do it suddenly, if you look at yourself thinking all of a sudden, spontaneously, unexpectedly, you will notice that nine times out of ten you are thinking something unpleasant. It is very rarely that you are thinking about harmonious, beautiful, constructive, happy things, full of hope, light and joy; you will see, try the experiment. Suddenly stop and look at yourself thinking, just like that: put a screen in front of your thought and look at yourself thinking, off-hand, you will see this at least nine times out of ten, and perhaps more. . . .

Say you have the slightest thing wrong with you; if you think of your body, it is always with the idea that something bad is going to happen to it — because when everything goes well, you don't think about it! . . .

Whereas Coué recommended... It was in this way that he cured his patients — he was a doctor: he would tell them, "You are going to repeat to yourself: 'I am getting better, little by little I am getting better' and again, 'I am strong, I am in good health and I can do this, I can do that.'"

I knew someone who was losing her hair disastrously, by handfuls. Someone got her to try this method. When she combed her hair she made herself think, "My hair will not fall out." The first time, the second time, it didn't work; but she continued and each time before combing her hair she would repeat with insistence, "I am going to comb my hair, but it won't fall out." And within a month her hair stopped falling. Later she again continued thinking, "Now my hair will grow." And she succeeded so well that I saw her with a magnificent head of hair. It was she herself who told me this, that this was what she had done after being on the point of becoming bald.

It is very, very effective. Only, while one is making the formation, another part of the mind must not say, "Oh, I am making a formation and it won't succeed", because in that way you undo your own work.[16]

The Secret of Coué's Method

Sri Aurobindo: The suggestions that create illness or unhealthy conditions of the physical being come usually through the subconscient — for a great part of the physical being, the most material part, is subconscient, that is to say, it has an obscure consciousness of its own but so obscure and shut up in itself that the mind does not know its movements or what is going on there. But all the same it is a consciousness and can receive suggestions from Forces outside, just as the mind and vital do. If it were not so, there would not be any possibility of opening it to the Force and the Force curing it; for without this consciousness in it it would not be able to respond. In Europe and America there are many people now who recognise this fact and treat their illnesses by making conscious mental suggestions to the body which counteract the obscure secret suggestions of illness in the subconscient. There was a famous Doctor in France who cured thousands of people by making them persistently put such counter-suggestions upon the body. That proves that illness has not a purely material cause, but is due to a disturbance of the secret consciousness in the body.[17]

These auto-suggestions — it is really faith in a mental form — act both on the subliminal and the subconscient. In the subliminal they set in action the powers of the inner being, its occult power to make thought, will or simple conscious force effective on the body — in the subconscient they silence or block the suggestions of death and illness (expressed or unexpressed) that prevent the return of health. They help also to combat the same things (adverse suggestions) in the mind, vital, body consciousness. Where all this is completely done or with some completeness, the effects can be very remarkable.[18]

The body consents [to an illness] from habit and from belief in the illness even though it suffers from it, and once started the illness runs its habitual course unless it is cut short by some strong counteracting force. If once the body can withdraw its consent, the illness immediately or quickly ceases, — that was the secret of the Coué system.[19]

How is Coué's method useful for the Sadhak of our yoga?

It may be used to a certain extent in the beginning but not to the end. His method is not universal. It does not succeed in all cases. In fact, it depends upon hypnotising the unconscious. But in some people's case the unconscious refuses the suggestion, so it does not succeed.

In our yoga we have to grow more and more conscious, so that the subconscious also, in our case, becomes wide-awake. Besides, the aim of our yoga is not to find out the most efficient method of healing diseases so much as to change the entire consciousness — even the physical — in order that disease may not come at all. The entire being must be so transformed that disease becomes impossible.[20]

Faith, Mental Effort and the Body

Mother, by a mental effort — for instance, the resolution not to take medicines when one is ill — can one succeed in making the body understand?

The Mother: That is not enough. A mental resolution is not enough, no. There are subtle reactions in your body which do not obey the mental resolution, it is not enough. Something else is needed.

There must be a contact with other regions. A power higher than the mind's is needed.

And from this point of view, everything in the mind is always subject to inner questioning. You take a resolution, but you can be sure something will always intrude which perhaps will not openly oppose this resolution, but will throw doubt on its effectiveness. It is enough for it to be subject to the slightest doubt for the resolution to lose half its effect. If at the same time as you say "I want", there is somewhere, silently lurking behind, in the background, something which asks itself, "What will the result be?", that is enough to ruin everything.

This play of the mind's working is extremely subtle and no ordinary human means can succeed in controlling it perfectly. . . .

A mental silence strong enough to prevent all outer vibrations from entering is indispensable. Well, that is something so difficult to achieve that one must really have passed from what Sri Aurobindo calls "the lower hemisphere" to the higher, exclusively spiritual hemisphere, for it not to happen.

No, it is not in the mental domain that victories are won. It is impossible. It is open to all influences, all contradictory currents. All the mental constructions one makes carry with them their own contradiction. One can try to override it or make it as harmless as possible, but it exists, it is there, and at the slightest weakness, lack of vigilance or inadvertence, it enters and destroys all the work. Mentally one achieves very few results, and they are always mixed. Something else is needed. You must pass from the mind into the domain of faith, or of a higher consciousness, to be able to act safely.

It is obvious that one of the most powerful means of acting on the body is faith. People who have a simple heart, not a very complicated mind — simple people, you know, who do not have a very great, very complicated mental development, but have a very intense faith — these have a good deal of power over their bodies, a good deal. That is why one is surprised sometimes: "Here is a man with a great realisation, an exceptional being, and he is enslaved to the smallest physical things, while that one, why, he is such a simple man and seems so uncouth, but he has a great faith, and he passes through difficulties and obstacles like a conqueror!"

I do not say that a highly cultured man cannot have faith, but it is more difficult, for there is always this mental element which contradicts, argues, tries to understand, which is difficult to convince, which wants proofs. His faith is less pure. It is necessary, then, to pass on to a higher degree in the evolutionary spiral, pass from the mental to the spiritual; then, naturally, faith takes on a quality of a very high order. But I mean that in daily life, ordinary life, a very simple man who has a very ardent faith can have a mastery over his body — without it being truly a "mastery"; it is simply a spontaneous movement — a control over his body far greater than someone who has reached a much higher development.[21]

Can mere faith create all, conquer all?

Yes, but it must be an integral faith and it must be absolute. And it must be of the right kind, not merely a force of mental thought or will, but something more and deeper. The will put forth by the mind sets up opposite reactions and creates a resistance. You must have heard something of the method of Coué in healing diseases. He knew some secret of this power and utilised it with considerable effect; but he called it imagination and his method gave the faith he called up too mental a form. Mental faith is not sufficient; it must be completed and enforced by a vital and even a physical faith, a faith of the body. If you can create in yourself an integral force of this kind in all your being, then nothing can resist it; but you must reach down to the most subconscious, you must fix the faith in the very cells of the body.[22]

Sri Aurobindo: I do not see how the method of faith in the cells can be likened to eating a slice of the moon. Nobody ever got a slice of the moon, but the healing by faith in the cells is an actual fact and a law of Nature and has been demonstrated often enough even apart from yoga. The way to get faith and all things else is to insist on having them and refuse to flag or despair or give up until one has them — it is the way by which everything has been got since this difficult earth began to have thinking and aspiring creatures upon it. It is to open always, always to the Light and turn one's back on the Darkness. It is to refuse the voices that say persistently, "You cannot, you shall not, you are incapable, you are the puppet of a dream," — for these are the enemy voices, they cut one off from the result that was coming by their strident clamour and then triumphantly point to the barrenness of the result as a proof of their thesis. The difficulty of the endeavour is a known thing, but the difficult is not the impossible — it is the difficult that has always been accomplished and the conquest of difficulties makes up all that is valuable in the earth's history.[23]

3

Detaching the Mind

Sri Aurobindo: The body consciousness through old habit of consciousness admits the force of illness and goes through the experiences which are associated with it — e.g., congestion of phlegm in the chest and feeling of suffocation or difficulty of breathing etc. To get rid of that one must awaken a will and consciousness in the body itself that refuses to allow these things to impose themselves upon it. But to get that, still more to get it completely is difficult. One step towards it is to get the inner consciousness separate from the body — to feel that it is not you who are ill, but it is only something taking place in the body and affecting your consciousness. It is then possible to see this separate body consciousness, what it feels, what are its reactions to things, how it works. One can then act on it to change its consciousness and reactions.[24]

We shall find, if we try, that the mind has this power of detachment and can stand back from the body not only in idea, but in act and as it were physically or rather vitally. This detachment of the mind must be strengthened by a certain attitude of indifference to the things of the body; we must not care essentially about its sleep or its waking, its movement or its rest, its pain or its pleasure, its health or ill-health, its vigour or its fatigue, its comfort or its discomfort, or what it eats or drinks. This does not mean that we shall not keep the body in right order so far as we can; we have not to fall into violent asceticisms or a positive neglect of the physical frame. But we have not either to be affected in mind by hunger or thirst or discomfort or ill-health or attach the importance which the physical and vital man attaches to the things of the body, or indeed any but a quite subordinate and purely instrumental importance. Nor must this instrumental importance be allowed to assume the proportions of a necessity; we must not for instance imagine that the purity of the mind depends on the things we eat or drink, although during a certain stage restrictions in eating and drinking are useful to our inner progress; nor on the other hand must we continue to think that the dependence of the mind or even of the life on food and drink is anything more than a habit, a customary relation which Nature has set up between these principles. As a matter of fact the food we take can be reduced by contrary habit and new relation to a minimum without the mental or vital vigour being in any way reduced; even on the contrary with a judicious development they can be trained to a greater potentiality of vigour by learning to rely on the secret fountains of mental and vital energy with which they are connected more than upon the minor aid of physical aliments. . . .

Release from Subjection to the Body

Thus disciplined the mind will gradually learn to take up towards the body the true attitude of the Purusha. First of all, it will know the mental Purusha as the upholder of the body and not in any way the body itself; for it is quite other than the physical existence which it upholds by the mind through the agency of the vital force. This will come to be so much the normal attitude of the whole being to the physical frame that the latter will feel to us as if something external and detachable like the dress we wear or an instrument we happen to be carrying in our hand. We may even come to feel that the body is in a certain sense non-existent except as a sort of partial expression of our vital force and of our mentality. These experiences are signs that the mind is coming to a right poise regarding the body, that it is exchanging the false view-point of the mentality obsessed and captured by physical sensation for the view-point of the true truth of things.

Secondly, with regard to the movements and experiences of the body the mind will come to know the Purusha seated within it as, first, the witness or observer of the movements and, secondly, the knower or perceiver of the experiences. It will cease to consider in thought or feel in sensation these movements and experiences as its own but rather consider and feel them as not its own, as operations of Nature governed by the qualities of Nature and their interaction upon each other. This detachment can be made so normal and carried so far that there will be a kind of division between the mind and the body and the former will observe and experience the hunger, thirst, pain, fatigue, depression, etc. of the physical being as if they were experiences of some other person with whom it has so close a *rapport* as to be aware of all that is going on within him. This division is a great means, a great step towards mastery; for the mind comes to observe these things first without being overpowered and finally without being at all affected by them, dispassionately, with clear understanding but with perfect detachment. This is the initial liberation of the mental being from servitude to the body; for by right knowledge put steadily into practice liberation comes inevitably.

Mastery of Mind over Body

Finally, the mind will come to know the Purusha in the mind as the master of Nature whose sanction is necessary to her movements. It will find that as the giver of the sanction he can withdraw the original fiat from the previous habits of Nature and that eventually the habit will cease or change in the direction indicated by the will of the Purusha; not at once, for the old sanction persists as an obstinate consequence of the past Karma of Nature until that is exhausted, and a good deal also depends on the force of the habit and the idea of fundamental necessity which the mind had previously attached to it; but if it is not one of the fundamental habits Nature has established for the relation of the mind, life and body and if the old sanction is not renewed by the mind or the habit willingly indulged, then eventually the change will come. Even the habit of hunger and thirst can be minimised, inhibited, put away; the habit of disease can be similarly minimised and gradually eliminated and in the meantime the power of the mind to set right the disorders of the body whether by conscious manipulation of vital force or by simple mental fiat will immensely increase. By a similar process the habit by which the bodily nature associates certain forms and degrees of activity with strain, fatigue, incapacity can be rectified and the power, freedom, swiftness, effectiveness of the work whether physical or mental which can be done with this bodily instrument marvellously increased, doubled, tripled, decupled.

. . . We have to correct the false notions popularised by materialistic Science. According to this Science the normal mental and physical states and the relations between mind and body actually established by our past evolution are the right, natural and healthy conditions and anything other, anything opposite to them is either morbid and wrong or a hallucination, self-deception and insanity. Needless to say, this conservative principle is entirely ignored by Science itself when it so diligently and successfully improves on the normal operations of physical Nature for the greater mastery of Nature by man. Suffice it to say here once for all that a change of mental and physical state and of relations between the mind and body which increases the purity and freedom of the being, brings a clear joy and peace and multiplies the power of the mind over itself and over the physical functions, brings about in a word man's greater mastery of his own nature, is obviously not morbid and cannot be considered a hallucination or self-deception since its effects are patent and positive. In fact, it is simply a willed advance of Nature in her evolution of the individual, an evolution which she will carry out in any case but in which she chooses to utilise the human will as her chief agent, because her essential aim is to lead the Purusha to conscious mastery over herself.[25]

The most we can do in the physical field by physical means is necessarily insecure as well as bound by limits; even what seems a perfect health and strength of the body is precarious and can be broken down at any moment by fluctuations from within or by a strong attack or shock from outside: only by the breaking of our limitations can a higher and more enduring perfection come. One direction in which our consciousness must grow is an increasing hold from within or from above on the body and its powers and its more conscious response to the higher parts of our being. . . . If the mind can take up and control the instincts and automatisms of the life-energy and the subtle physical consciousness and the body, if it can enter into them, consciously use and, as we may say, fully mentalise their instinctive or spontaneous action, the perfection of these energies, their action too become more conscious and more aware of themselves and more perfect. But it is necessary for the mind too to grow in perfection and this it can do best when it depends less on the fallible intellect of physical mind, when it is not limited even by the more orderly and accurate working of the reason and can grow in intuition and acquire a wider, deeper and closer seeing and the more luminous drive of energy of a higher intuitive will. Even within the limits of its present evolution it is difficult to measure the degree to which the mind is able to extend its control or its use of the body's powers and capacities and when the mind rises to higher powers still and pushes back its human boundaries, it becomes impossible to fix any limits: even, in certain realisations, an intervention by the will in the automatic working of the bodily organs seems to become possible.

Wherever limitations recede and in proportion as they recede, the body becomes a more plastic and responsive and in that measure a more fit and perfect instrument of the action of the spirit.[26]

4

Neutralising Pain

The Mother: You may have been told that certain bodily complaints will give you a great deal of pain. Things like that are often said. You then make a formation of fear and keep expecting the pain. And the pain comes even when it need not.

But in case it is there after all, I can tell you one thing. If the consciousness is turned upward, the pain vanishes. If it is turned downward, the pain is felt and even increases. When one experiments with the upward and the downward turnings, one sees that the bodily complaint as such has nothing to do with the pain. The body may suffer very much or not at all, although its condition is exactly the same. It is the turn of the consciousness that makes all the difference.

I say "turned upward" because to turn towards the Divine is the best method, but what can be said in general is that if the consciousness is turned away from the pain to one's work or anything that interests one, the pain ceases.

And not only the pain but whatever damage there may be in an organ is set right much more easily when the consciousness is taken away from the trouble and one is open to the Divine. There is the Sat aspect of the Divine — the pure supreme Existence above or beyond or behind the cosmos. If you can keep in contact with it, all physical complaints can be removed.[27]

There is one thing you can try to do: it is not to concentrate on your pain, to turn your attention away as much as you can, not think at all of your pain, think of it as little as possible and above all not be concentrated on it, not pay attention

— "Oh, I am in pain", then it becomes a little worse; "Oh, I am in even greater pain", then it becomes still worse, like that, because you are concentrating on it. And this is the mistake one always makes: to think, be there, attentive, awaiting the sign of pain; then naturally it comes, it comes increased by the attention one has concentrated on it. That is why, when you are not well, the best thing to do is to read or have something read to you, depending on the condition you are in. But if you can turn your attention away, you no longer suffer.[28]

I am very much interested in writing and reading stories. Then I forget the pain.

Which proves that your pain is at least three-fourths imaginary.

Make me understand this imaginary illness. I don't understand it at all.

You think that you are ill and that increases the illness. When you forget the illness, it goes away almost completely.[29]

The only unfailing method for getting rid of illnesses is to turn one's attention away from them and refuse to give them any importance.[30]

Sri Aurobindo: Your ailment is evidently in its foundation an illness of the nerves, not an ordinary physical disease. These maladies . . . increase if anything in you assents to them and accepts them, and the more the mind gives value to them and dwells on them, the more they grow. The only way is to remain quiet, disassociate yourself and refuse to accept it or make much of it. . . . If you can acquire and keep patience and fortitude and the right consciousness and right attitude with regard to these things, the hold they have will progressively disappear.[31]

Eliminating the Mental Factor in Pain

The Mother: In the case of people who can avoid getting completely upset as soon as they have a pain somewhere, who manage to endure quietly, to keep their balance, it seems that the body's capacity to tolerate disorder without going to pieces increases. . . . The body can bear much more than we think, if no fear or anxiety is added to the pain. If we eliminate the mental factor, the body, left to itself, has neither fear nor apprehension nor anxiety about what is going to happen — no anguish — and it can bear a great deal.

The second step is when the body has decided to endure — it takes the decision to endure: immediately the acuteness, what is sharp in the pain disappears. I am speaking absolutely materially.

And if you are calm — here another factor intervenes, the need for inner calm — if you have this inner calm, then the pain changes into an almost pleasant sensation — not "pleasant" in the ordinary sense, but an almost comfortable feeling which comes. Again, I am speaking purely physically, materially.

And the last stage is when the cells have faith in the divine Presence and in the sovereign divine Will, when they have this trust that all is for the best; then comes ecstasy — the cells open, like this, become luminous and ecstatic.

That makes four stages. . . . The last is probably not within the reach of everyone, but the first three are very clear.[32]

Before reaching a higher state of consciousness, there is a stage where one can develop in oneself the faculty of reason — a clear, precise, logical reason, quite objective in its vision of things. . . . Most people, when something troubles them, become very unreasonable. For example, when they are sick, they spend their time saying, "Oh, how sick I am, how awful it is! Is it going to be like this all the time?" And naturally it gets worse and worse. Or when some misfortune happens to them, they cry out: "It is only to me that these things happen! And I thought everything was fine before", and they burst into a fit of tears, a fit of nerves. Well, not to speak of superman, in man himself there is a higher capacity called reason, which is able to look at things calmly, coolly, reasonably. And this reason tells you, "Don't worry, that will improve nothing; you must not complain, you must accept the thing since it has happened." Then you calm down at once. It is a very good mental training; it develops judgment, vision, objectivity, and at the same time it has a very healthy effect on your character. It allows you to avoid making yourself ridiculous by giving in to your nerves and lets you behave like a reasonable person.[33]

Sri Aurobindo: For knowledge, when it goes to the root of our troubles, has in itself a marvellous healing-power as it were. As soon as you touch the quick of the trouble, as soon as you, diving down and down, get at what really ails you, the pain disappears as though by a miracle.[34]

Cutting the Connection

The Mother: When one is not too soft, when one has a little bit of endurance and decides within oneself not to pay too much attention, quite remarkably the pain diminishes. And there are a number of illnesses or states of physical disequilibrium which can be cured simply by removing the effect, that is, by stopping the suffering. Usually it comes back, because

V8

the cause is still there. If you find the cause of the illness and act directly on its cause, then you can be cured radically. But if you are not able to do that, you can make use of this influence, of this control over pain in order — by suppressing or eliminating the pain or mastering it in yourself — to have an effect on the illness. So this is an effect, so to say, from outside inwards; while the other is an effect from within outwards, which is much more lasting and much more complete. But the first way is also effective.

... There are people who are more or less what I call "soft", that is, unable to take pain, to endure it, who immediately say, "I can't! It is unbearable. I can't endure any more!" Ah, that does not help the situation; it does not stop their suffering, because it is not by telling it you don't want it that you make it go away! But if you can ... bring into yourself a sort of immobility, as total as possible, in the place that is suffering, this has the effect of an anaesthetic. If you succeed in bringing an inner immobility, an immobility of the inner vibration, at the spot where you are suffering, it has exactly the same effect as an anaesthetic. It cuts the contact between the place that is suffering and the brain, and once you have cut the contact, if you can keep this state long enough, the pain will disappear. You must form the habit of doing this. But you get the chance, all the time you get the chance to do it: you cut yourself, knock into something, you know, one is always getting little bruises somewhere — especially when doing athletics, gymnastics and so on — well, these are opportunities which are given to us. Instead of sitting there observing the pain, trying to analyse it, concentrating on it, which makes it increase more and more ... you deliberately make this kind of concentration of immobility in the suffering nerve; at the point where the pain is, you induce as total an immobility as you can. Well, you will see that it works, as I told you, like an anaesthetic: it puts it to sleep. And then, if you can add to that a kind of inner peace and a confidence that the pain will go away, well, I assure you it will go.

Of all things, what is considered the most difficult from

the yogic point of view is toothache, because it is very close to the brain. Well, I know that this can be done to the point of truly not feeling the pain at all; this does not cure the bad tooth, but there are cases in which one can succeed in killing the painful nerve. Usually in a tooth it is the nerve that has been attacked by the caries, by the disease, and begins to protest with all its might. So if you can manage to establish this immobility there, you prevent it from vibrating, you prevent it from protesting. And what is remarkable is that if you do it constantly enough, with enough perseverance, the sick nerve will die and you will not suffer at all any more. Because that is what was suffering and when it is dead it no longer suffers. Try. I hope you never have a toothache![35]

The first thing and the most indispensable is to nullify the pain by cutting the connection. . . .

For example, you have cut your finger, there is a nerve that has been affected, and so the nerve runs quickly to tell the brain, up there, that something has happened, has gone wrong down here. That is what gives you pain, to awaken your attention, to tell you: "You know, there is something wrong." So the mind immediately gets worried: "What is wrong? Oh! how it hurts", etc., etc. — then turns to the finger and tries to take care of what is still intact. Usually one puts a small bandage. But to keep from having pain if it hurts very much, you must simply cut the connection with your mind, saying to the nerve, "Now keep quiet, you have done your work, you have warned me, you don't need to say anything more; ploff! I am stopping you." And when this is done well, you don't suffer any more, it is finished, the pain is completely stopped. That is the best thing. It is infinitely better than telling yourself it is painful.[36]

Going out of the Body

When one is in much pain or discomfort, how can one sleep peacefully?

The Mother: This takes a certain yogic power. The best way — and this one is absolute — is to go out of your body.

When the body is suffering, when you have a fever or are feeling sick, or when the body is quite ill, the only thing to do is to come out of it, to bring out your vital being. And then, if you are a yogi and know how, you rise just above, so as to see your body. The vital being, if it has come out in a fairly material form, can see the body — you see your own physical body. And then at that moment, with the consciousness you have and the force you have, you can direct the rays of your forces on the place in the body which is ill. But this is the peak. It is the surest way to cure oneself, and if one has the power and the knowledge it is infallible.

You can cure yourself of anything whatever in a very short time. Only, all this means a lot of practice, a training of the being. It cannot be done on the spur of the moment. But in fact when the pain is intolerable and people faint, they do this instinctively. To faint is to go out of your body. Well, there are people who are not too closely tied to their body, and when something goes wrong, is too painful or they are not well, they faint.

Too great a pain makes you faint, that is, you go out of your body, you really go out and leave the body very inert; and, provided someone is there who has enough knowledge not to shake you like this (*gesture*) to wake you up, it is a way to escape from suffering. Of course, if you have beside you someone who is panic-stricken and sprinkles cold water on your head or shakes you, then the result can be disastrous, but otherwise one can... And little by little, naturally, as there is no longer any consciousness there to record the suffering, everything becomes calm, and in almost every case the body becomes motionless enough to be able to rest even in spite of the suffering. It doesn't feel it at all any more. This is the best way.[37]

Moving the Centre of Awareness

The Mother: The mental force, mental activity is independent of the brain. We are in the habit of using the brain but we can use something else or rather, concentrate the mental force elsewhere, and have the impression that our mental activity comes from there. One can concentrate one's mental force in the solar plexus, here (*gesture*), and feel the mental activity coming out from there. . . .

If ever you have a headache I advise you to do this: to take the thought-force, the mental force — and even if you can draw a little of your vital force, that too — and make it come down, like this (*gesture of very slowly sliding both hands from the top of the head downwards*). If you have a headache or congestion or a touch of sunstroke, for instance, in any case something has happened to you, well, if you know how to do this and bring down the force here, like this, here (*showing the centre of the chest*), or even lower down (*showing the stomach*), well, it will disappear. It will disappear. You will be able to do this in five minutes. You can try, the next time you have a headache.... I hope you won't have a headache but the next time you do, try this. . . .

So, sit quite at ease and then take all your force as though you were taking, you see... all the energy in your head, take it and then make it come down, down, down, like this, slowly, very carefully, right down here, down to the navel. And you will see that your headache will disappear. I have made the experiment many times.... It is a very good remedy, very easy; there is no need to take pills or injections; it gets cured like that.[38]

Widening Oneself

The Mother: When you have to face anguish, suffering, revolt, pain or a feeling of helplessness — whatever it may be, all the things that come to you on the way and are precisely the difficulties you have to overcome — if you can physically, that is to say in your bodily consciousness, have the impression of widening yourself, of unfolding yourself, one might say — you feel like something all folded up, one fold on another, like a piece of cloth, you know, which is folded and refolded and folded again — well, if you have this impression that what is gripping and squeezing you and making you suffer or paralysing your movement is like a too closely, too tightly folded piece of cloth or like a parcel that is too well tied, too well packed, and that slowly, little by little, you undo all the folds and stretch yourself out exactly as one unfolds a piece of cloth or a sheet of paper and spreads it out flat, and you lie flat and make yourself very wide, as wide as possible, spreading yourself out as far as you can, opening yourself and stretching out in an attitude of complete passivity with what I might call "the face to the light", not curling back upon your difficulty, doubling up on it, shutting it into yourself, so to speak, but on the contrary unfurling yourself as much as you can, as perfectly as you can, putting the difficulty before the Light — the Light that comes from above — if you do that in all the domains, and even if mentally you don't succeed in doing it — for it is sometimes difficult — if you can imagine yourself doing it *physically*, almost materially, well, when you have finished unfolding yourself and stretching yourself out, you will find that more than three-quarters of the difficulty is gone. And then just a little work of receptivity to the Light and the last quarter will disappear.[39]

You must widen your consciousness, if you can.
I knew someone who wanted to widen his consciousness

and said he had found a way: it was to lie on his back at night, out of doors, and look at the stars and try to identify himself with them and go out there into an immense world, and so lose all sense of proportion on the order of the earth and all these small things and become as vast as the sky — you cannot say as vast as the universe, for we see only a tiny part of it, but as vast as the sky with all the stars. And then, you know, the little impurities fall away for the time being and you understand things on a very large scale. It is a good exercise.[40]

Sweet Mother, how can we make our consciousness vast?

Vast? Ah, there are many ways of doing that.

The easiest way is to identify yourself with something vast. For instance, when you feel that you are shut up in a completely narrow and limited thought, will, consciousness, when you feel as though you were in a shell, then if you begin thinking about something very vast, like, for example, the immensity of the waters of an ocean, and if you really think of this ocean and how it stretches out far, far, far, far, in all directions, like this (*Mother stretches out her arms*), how, in relation to you, it is so far, so far that you cannot see its shores, you cannot reach its end anywhere, neither behind nor in front nor to the left nor to the right... it is wide, wide, wide, wide.... You think of that, and then you have the impression that you are floating on this sea, like that, and that there are *no* limits.... This is very easy. So you widen your consciousness a little. . . .

There are lots of intellectual ways to widen one's consciousness. . . . When you are troubled by something, when something is painful or very unpleasant for you, if you begin to think of the eternity of time and the immensity of space, if you think of all that has gone before and all that will come hereafter, and that this second in eternity is truly just a passing breath, and that it seems so utterly ridiculous to be upset by something which in the eternity of time is... there is not even time to notice it, it has no place, no importance, because what is a second in eternity?... if you can manage to realise this, to... how to put it?... visualise, picture the little person you are, on the little earth where you are, and the little second of consciousness which for the moment is hurting you or is unpleasant for you — which is itself only a second in your existence — and that you yourself have been many things before and will be many more things afterwards, that what affects you now you will probably have completely forgotten in ten years, or if you remember it you will say, "How is it that I attached any importance to that?"... if you can first realise that, and then think of your little person which is a second in eternity — not even a second: imperceptible, a fraction of a second in eternity — that the whole world has unrolled before this and will continue to unroll indefinitely, in front, behind, and that... well, then suddenly you sense the utter absurdity of the importance you attach to what has happened to you. *Truly* you feel... how ridiculous it is to attach any importance to your life, to yourself, and to what happens to you. And in the space of three minutes, if you do this properly, all unpleasantness is swept away. Even a very deep pain can be swept away. Simply a concentration like this, placing yourself in infinity and eternity. Everything goes away. You come out of it cleansed. . . . It immediately takes you out of your little ego.[41]

5

Quietude and Peace

The Mother: The imperative condition for cure is calm and quietness. Any agitation, any narrowness prolongs the illness.[42]

One must find the inner peace and keep it constantly. In the force this peace brings, all these little miseries will disappear.[43]

To relieve tension, ten minutes of *real calm*, inner and outer, are more effective than all the remedies in the world. In silence lies the most effective help.[44]

You cannot sleep because your mind is not quiet. Your health is bad because your mind is not quiet. So there is only one remedy to all your ills: *quiet your mind.*[45]

Quieting the Mind

The Mother: It is obvious that when I tell someone, "Be calm", I may mean many different things according to the person. But the first indispensable calm is mental quietude, for generally that is the one that is most lacking. When I tell someone, "Be calm", I mean: try not to have restless, excited, agitated thoughts; try to calm your brain and to stop turning around in all your imaginations and observations and mental constructions. . . .

For each the method is different, but *first* one must feel for whatever reason — whether because one is tired or because one is overstrained or because one wants truly to rise beyond the state one is living in — one must first understand and feel the need for this quietude, this peace in the mind. And then, afterwards, one may try out successively all the methods, old and new, to attain the result. . . .

Quietude is a very positive state; there is a positive peace which is not merely the opposite of conflict — an active peace, contagious, powerful, which controls and calms, puts things in order, organises. This is what I am talking about. When I tell someone, "Be calm", I don't mean to say, "Go and sleep, be inert and passive, and don't do anything", far from it!... True quietude is a very great force, a very great strength.[46]

How can one establish a settled peace and silence in the mind?

First of all, you must want it.

And then you must try, and you must persevere, keep trying. . . . You sit quietly, to begin with; and then, instead of thinking of fifty things, start saying to yourself, "Peace, peace, peace, peace, peace, calm, peace...." You imagine peace and calm. You aspire, ask it to come: "Peace, peace, calm." And then, when something comes and tries to touch you and be active, you say quietly, like this: "Peace, peace, peace." Do not look at the thoughts, do not listen to the thoughts, you understand. You must not pay attention to everything that comes. You know, when someone bores you terribly and you want to get rid of him, you don't listen to him, do you? Good! You turn your head away and think of something else. Well, you must do that: when thoughts come, you must not look at them, not listen to them, not pay any attention at all, you must behave as though they did not exist. And then, repeat all the time like a kind of... how shall I put it?... as an idiot does, who always repeats the same thing. Well, you must do the same; you must repeat, "Peace, peace, peace." So you try this for a few minutes and then do what you have to do; and then, another time, you begin again; you sit down again and then you try. Do this on getting up in the morning, do it in the evening when going to bed. You can do it... say you want to digest your food well, you can do this for a few minutes before eating. You cannot imagine how much it will help your digestion! Before beginning to eat, you sit quietly for a while and say, "Peace, peace, peace..." and everything becomes calm. It is as if all the noises were going far, far, far away.... (*Mother stretches out her arms on both sides*) And then you must continue doing this; and there comes a time when you no longer need to sit down, and no matter what you are doing, no matter what you are saying, it is always "Peace, peace, peace." Everything remains here, like this, it does not enter (*gesture in front of the forehead*), it remains like this. And then one is always in a perfect peace... after some years.

But at the beginning, a very small beginning, two or three minutes; it is very simple. For something complicated you have to make an effort, and when you make an effort you are not quiet. It is hard to make an effort while remaining quiet. Very simple, very simple, one must be very simple in these things. It is as if you were learning to call a friend: he comes because he is called. Well, make peace and calm your friends and call them: "Come, peace, peace, peace, peace, come!"[47]

Always it is as though I was enveloping you in a cocoon of Peace. And then, if you could put — precisely into this mind which vibrates, stirs all the time, just like a monkey — if you could put there... it is a Peace that acts *directly* in this material vibration — a Peace in which everything relaxes.

Do not think, do not think of trying to transform this

physical mind or to silence or abolish it; all that is still activity. Simply let it go on, but... put the Peace, feel the Peace, live the Peace, know the Peace, Peace, Peace....
    That is the only thing.[48]

Making Oneself Blank

What are the forces that are in operation when one is in silent meditation?

The Mother: It depends upon the one who meditates.

But in silent meditation does he not make himself a complete blank? Then how can anything depend upon him?

Even if you make yourself an absolute blank, that does not change the nature of your aspiration. . . . On the quality of the aspiration depends the force that answers and the work that it comes to do. To make yourself blank in meditation creates an inner silence; it does not mean that you have become nothing or have become a dead and inert mass. Making yourself an empty vessel, you invite that which shall fill it. It means that you release the stress of your inner consciousness towards realisation. The nature of the consciousness and the degree of its stress determine the forces that you bring into play and whether they shall help and fulfil or fail or even harm and hinder.[49]

We may take the example . . . you have a chronic illness, a deformity of the body, a physical defect. So your consciousness, in its aspiration and will, puts a more or less constant stress on the thing it wants to realise, what you want to cure. Well, when you make yourself blank within in meditation (this is one form of meditation, if you like), it means that you stop this concentration of will: your consciousness becomes neutral for the time being. Its stress is upon this point (it may be on other points, on things more or less concrete or abstract, but the stress is on one point) and when you make yourself blank you withdraw this pressure, this stress, and remain like a white page on which nothing is written. This is what I call "making yourself blank": not to have an active will concentrated on one point or another. And so I say the moment you make yourself blank, in effect the stress is stopped, and yet in your silent aspiration you put yourself in contact with the forces attracted by the stress you ordinarily have, the special point on which you insist at other times. That is why I have emphasised the fact that all depends upon the person, because everything depends upon his habitual aspiration, the thing he normally wants to realise; for he is naturally in contact with the forces that will respond to his aspiration. So if for a certain time one stops the activity of this aspiration and remains in a silent, passive receptivity, well, the effect of the habitual aspiration remains and will draw just the forces that should respond to it.[50]

Bringing Peace into the Body

The Mother: This feeling of something so still — but not closed, still but open, still but receptive — is something which becomes established through repeated experiences. There is a great difference between a silence that is dead, dull, unresponsive and the receptive silence of a quieted mind. . . .

They have an effect, all these things have an effect on the functioning of the body — the functioning of the organs, of the brain, of the nerves, etc.[51]

The only thing I can suggest about diseases is to call down peace. Keep the mind away from the body by whatever means

— whether by reading Sri Aurobindo's books or meditation. It is in this state that the Grace acts. And it is the Grace alone that cures. The medicines only give a faith to the body. That is all.[52]

For your ill-health, do not forget to try to bring down the Divine Peace. Because no illness can resist the Peace of the Lord, and even to remember and to try will give you some relief.[53]

Peace and stillness are the great remedy for disease. When we can bring peace in our cells we are cured.[54]

Is the consciousness of the Divine possible in even the physical cells?

Sri Aurobindo: Yes, the cells can have peace and joy and other things. When they are quite conscious, they can throw opposing forces out. When peace descends into the physical being, it is a great force for cure. . . .

There is an infinite sea of peace, power, Ananda just above the head — what we call "overhead". And if one is in contact with it one can get these things always.[55]

6

Change of Consciousness

The Mother: Every time one has the feeling of having won a victory, one finds out that this victory was incomplete, partial, fugitive. . . .

This is very apparent, very noticeable in physical conquests over the body. Through a very assiduous labour one succeeds in overcoming a weakness, a limitation, a bad habit, and one believes this is a definitive victory; but after some time or at times immediately one realises that nothing is completely done, nothing is definitive, that what one thought to have accomplished has to be done again. For only a total change of consciousness and the intervention of a new force, a reversal of consciousness can make the victory complete. . . .

The entire consciousness must be changed, a reversal of consciousness must be achieved, a springing up out of the state one is in towards a higher state from which one looks down on all the weaknesses one wants to cure, and from which one has a comprehensive vision of the work to be accomplished.[56]

The ordinary human consciousness, even in the most developed, even in men of great talent and great realisation, is a movement turned outwards — all the energies are directed outwards, the whole consciousness is spread outwards; and if anything is turned inwards, it is very little, very rare, very fragmentary, it happens only under the pressure of very special circumstances, violent shocks, the shocks life gives precisely with the intention of slightly reversing this movement of exteriorisation of the consciousness.

But all who have lived a spiritual life have had the same experience: all of a sudden something in their being has been reversed, so to speak, has been turned suddenly and sometimes completely inwards, and also at the same time upwards, from within upwards — but it is not an external "above", it is within, deep, something other than the heights as they are physically conceived. Something has literally been turned over. There has been a decisive experience and the standpoint in life, the way of looking at life, the attitude one takes in relation to it, has suddenly changed, and in some cases quite definitively, irrevocably.[57]

Indeed, what better use could one make of an illness than to take the opportunity to go deep within oneself and awaken, take birth into a new consciousness, more luminous and more true.[58]

Consciousness, Mind and Body

Sri Aurobindo: It is becoming always clearer that not only does the capacity of our total consciousness far exceed that of our organs, the senses, the nerves, the brain, but that even for our ordinary thought and consciousness these organs are only their habitual instruments and not their generators. Consciousness uses the brain which its upward strivings have produced, brain has not produced nor does it use the consciousness. There are even abnormal instances which go to prove that our organs are not entirely indispensable instruments, — that the heart-beats are not absolutely essential to life, any more than is breathing, nor the organised brain-cells to thought. Our physical organism no more causes or explains thought and consciousness than the construction of an engine causes or explains the motive-power of steam or electricity. The force is anterior, not the physical instrument.[59]

Consciousness is usually identified with mind, but mental consciousness is only the human range which no more exhausts all the possible ranges of consciousness than human sight exhausts all the gradations of colour or human hearing all the gradations of sound — for there is much above or below that is to man invisible and inaudible. So there are ranges of consciousness above and below the human range, with which the normal human has no contact and they seem to it unconscious, — supramental or overmental and submental ranges.[60]

It all depends upon where the consciousness places itself and concentrates itself. If the consciousness places or concentrates itself within the ego, you are identified with the ego — if in the mind, it is identified with the mind and its activities and so on. If the consciousness puts its stress outside, it is said to live in the external being and becomes oblivious of its inner mind and vital and inmost psychic; if it goes inside, puts its centralising stress there, then it knows itself as the inner being or, still deeper, as the psychic being; if it ascends out of the body to the planes where self is naturally conscious of its wideness and freedom it knows itself as the Self and not the mind, life or body. It is this stress of consciousness that makes all the difference.[61]

The Mother: The falsity of the consciousness naturally has material consequences... and that is what illness is! ... When you are open and in contact with the Divine, the vibration gives you strength, energy; and if you are quiet enough, it fills you with great joy — and all of this in the cells of the body. You fall back into the ordinary consciousness and straight away, without anything changing, the *same* thing, the *same* vibration coming from the *same* source turns into a pain, an uneasiness, a feeling of uncertainty, instability and decrepitude.[62]

All is in the Divine and all is divine. And necessarily, if you change your state of consciousness and are identified with the Divine, that changes the very nature of things. For example, what seemed to cause pain or sorrow or misery is found to be, on the contrary, an opportunity for the Divine to grow closer to you, and you realise that from this event perhaps you may draw a still greater joy than that derived from something pleasant. Only it must be understood that way, in that spirit and with that consciousness, for otherwise, if taken in the ordinary sense, it is the very contradiction of the principle that all is divine.

The same thing, exactly the same vibration, according to the way you receive and respond to it, can bring either intense joy or considerable despair, exactly the same thing, according to the state of consciousness you are in. So there is nothing of which it could be said that it is a misfortune. There is nothing that can be called suffering. All you have to do is to change your state of consciousness. That is all.[63]

7

The Psychic Being

The Mother: One may have sufferings and not feel them, be as if they did not exist. That is, a misfortune . . . touches only the outer consciousness, the physical, the mental, the vital, but the psychic — in truth, the psychic is above all suffering. Let us take a very simple example: an illness. A physical disorder brings suffering, at times much suffering, but there are people who are in such a state of consciousness that their physical sufferings do not exist, they are not real for them.[64]

Sri Aurobindo: The inner being is composed of the inner mental, inner vital, inner physical, — but that is not the psychic being. The psychic is the inmost being and quite distinct from these. The word 'psychic' is indeed used in English to indicate anything that is other or deeper than the external mind, life and body, anything occult or supraphysical, but that is a use which brings confusion and error and we entirely discard it when we speak or write about yoga.[65]

If we learn to live within, we infallibly awaken to this presence within us which is our more real self, a presence profound, calm, joyous and puissant of which the world is not the master — a presence which, if it is not the Lord Himself, is the radiation of the Lord within. We are aware of it within supporting and helping the apparent and superficial self and smiling at its pleasures and pains as at the error and passion of a little child. And if we can go back into ourselves and identify ourselves, not with our superficial experience, but with that radiant penumbra of the Divine, we can live in that attitude towards the contacts of the world and, standing back in our entire consciousness from the pleasures and pains of the body, vital being and mind, possess them as experiences whose nature being superficial does not touch or impose itself on our core and real being.[66]

The Psychic Being and the Outer Consciousness

The Mother: There are many different reasons why one feels at times more alive, more full of strength and joy.... Generally speaking, in ordinary life there are people who, due to their very constitution, the way they are made, are in a certain harmony with Nature, as though they breathed with the same rhythm, and usually these people are always joyful, content, they succeed in what they do, they avoid many troubles and catastrophes; in short, they are those who are in harmony with the rhythm of life and Nature. And besides this, there are days when one is in contact with the divine Consciousness which is at work, with the Grace; and then everything is tinged, coloured with this Presence, and things which usually seem dull or uninteresting to you become charming, pleasant, attractive, instructive — *everything* lives and vibrates and is full of promise and force. So when you open to that, you feel stronger, freer, happier, full of energy, and everything has a meaning. You understand why things are as they are and you participate in the general movement.

There are other times when, for some reason, you are foggy or shut up in yourself or down in the dumps, and then you no longer feel anything and all things lose their taste, their interest, their value; you are like a walking block of wood.

Now, if you succeed in uniting consciously with your psychic being, you can *always* be in this state of receptivity, inner joy, energy, progress, communion with the divine Presence. And when you are in communion with That, you see it everywhere, in everything, and all things take on their true significance.

What does it depend on?... On an inner rhythm, perhaps a grace; in any case, a receptivity to something that is beyond you.[67]

Sri Aurobindo: The ease and peace are felt very deep and far within because they are in the psychic and the psychic is very deep within us, covered over by the mind and vital. When you meditate you open to the psychic, become aware of your psychic consciousness deep within and feel these things. In order that the ease and peace and happiness may become strong and stable and felt in all the being and in the body, you have to go still deeper within and bring out the full force of the psychic into the physical.[68]

The peace and spontaneous knowledge are in the psychic being and from there they spread to mind and vital and physical. It is in the outer physical consciousness that the difficulty still tries to persist and brings the restlessness sometimes into the physical mind, sometimes into the nerves, sometimes in the shape of bodily trouble into the body. But all these things can and must go. Even the illnesses can go entirely with the growth of peace and power in the nerves and physical cells — stomach pains, weakness of the eyes and everything else.[69]

Psychic Discernment and Physical Disorders

Sri Aurobindo: When the psychic being awakes then it is able to perceive the influence of the disease even before it enters the body. Not only does one perceive it, but one knows which organ is going to be attacked and one can keep off the attack with the help of the Higher Power.[70]

The Mother: It is only if you have formed the habit of going within yourself, of referring to the inner psychic consciousness and letting it decide in you what you will do, that you do it with certitude, without hesitation, without a question or anything. You know what is to be done and there is no room for argument. . . .

Otherwise, if you are in the habit of studying and observing, you have before you all the little things of life which repeat themselves constantly; you do not want to live mechanically any more by a kind of habit, you want to live consciously, making use of your will. Well, at every minute you are faced by a problem you cannot solve. I mean purely physically. Take a certain difficulty you have in your body — what we call a disorder — which is translated by a discomfort or an indisposition; it is not an illness, it is an indisposition, a discomfort, something is not functioning very well. Then if you do not have this psychic knowledge which makes you do directly the thing that should be done and without argument, if you want to refer it to your mind and to what you consider to be the knowledge you have, then... Take a case which lies in the field of medicine, that is, "Should I do this or that, take this medicine or that, change my diet, take this food or that?"... So you look into it. If you have never known more than a certain number of very elementary principles, your choice is easy enough. But if by chance you have studied a little and know, let us say, only the different systems of medical treatment... there are the systems of different countries, the different medical systems; there are, you know, allopathy, homeopathy, this and that. So one tells you one thing, another tells you another. You know people who have told you, "Do not do this, do that", others who say, "Above all do not do that, do this", and so on, and so you find yourself faced by the problem and ask yourself, "Well, with all that, what do I know, what am I going to decide? I know nothing."

There is only one thing that knows in you, it is your psychic; *that* makes no mistake, it will tell you immediately, instantaneously, and if you obey it without a word and without ideas and arguments, it will make you do the right thing. But as for all the rest... you are lost.[71]

Accidents and an Awakened Consciousness

The Mother: There is a moment for choice, even in an accident. For example, you slip and fall. Just between the moment you have slipped and the moment you fall, there is a fraction of a second. At that moment you have the choice: it may be nothing, it may be serious. Only, your consciousness must naturally be wide awake and you must be constantly in contact with your psychic being — you do not have time to make the contact, you must be in contact. Between the moment you slip and the moment you are on the ground, if the mental and psychic formation is strong enough, then it is nothing, nothing will happen — nothing happens. Whereas if at that moment the mind according to its habit becomes a pessimist and cries: "Oh! I have slipped!"... It lasts a fraction of a second, it doesn't take even a minute, it is a fraction of a second; during a fraction of a second you have the choice. But you must be so alert, every minute of your life! For a fraction of a second you have the choice; there is a fraction of a second when you can prevent the accident from being serious, when you can prevent the illness from entering into you. You always have the choice. But it is for a fraction of a second and you must not miss it. If you miss it, it is too late.

One can make it afterwards? (laughter)

No. Afterwards, there is another moment.... You have fallen, you have already hurt yourself; but there is still a moment when you can change things for the better or worse, so that it may be something very fugitive whose bad effects will quickly disappear, or something that becomes as serious, as critical as it can be. I don't know if you have noticed that there are people who never miss the chance for an accident. Every time there is the possibility of an accident, they have it. And never is their accident ordinary. Every time the accident can be serious, it is serious. Well, usually in life one says: "Oh! he has bad luck, he is unfortunate, really the dice are against him." But all that is ignorance. It depends absolutely on the working of one's consciousness. . . . There are people who could have been killed and they come out of it unscathed; there are others for whom it was not serious and it becomes serious.

But it does not depend on thought, on the ordinary working of the mind. They may apparently have thoughts as good as the others — it is not that. It is the second of choice — people who know how to react just in the right way at the right time. I could give you hundreds of examples. It is quite interesting.

It depends absolutely on character. Some have such an awakened consciousness, so alert, that they are never asleep, they are awake within. Just at the second it is needed they call the help. Or they invoke the divine Force. But just at the second it is needed. So the danger is averted, nothing happens. They could have been killed; they come out of it absolutely unhurt. With others, on the contrary, as soon as they have the slightest scratch, something in their being gets out of order: a sort of fear or pessimism or defeatism comes up automatically in their consciousness. It was nothing, they had just twisted their leg, and the next minute they break it. There is no reason for it. They could very well not have broken their leg.

There are others who climb up to the second storey on a ladder which gives way under them. They could have been dashed to the ground — they come out of it without being hurt in the least. How did they do it? It seems amazing, and yet this is how things happen to them. They find themselves lying on the ground quite all right; nothing has happened to them. I could give you the names, I am telling you precise facts. . . .

I knew someone who really should have died and did not die because of this. For his consciousness reacted very quickly.

He had taken poison by mistake: instead of taking one dose of a certain medicine, he had taken twelve and it was a poison; he should have died, the heart should have stopped (it was many years ago) and he is still quite alive! He reacted in the right way.

If these things were narrated they would be called miracles. They are not miracles: it is an awakened consciousness.[72]

Experiences of the Inner Being

Mother, how can one change one's consciousness?

The Mother: Naturally there are many ways, but each person must do it from the starting-point that is accessible to him; and the indication of the way usually comes spontaneously, through something like an unexpected experience. And for each one, it presents itself a little differently.

For instance, you may be aware of the ordinary consciousness, which is extended on the surface, horizontally, and works on a plane which is at the same time a surface of things and has a contact with the outer surface of things, people, circumstances; and then all of a sudden, for some reason — as I say, for each one it is different — there is a shifting upwards, and instead of seeing things horizontally, of being on the same level as they are, you suddenly rise superior to them and see them from above, in their totality, instead of seeing only a small number of things immediately next to you; it is as though something were drawing you above and making you see from a mountain-top or an airplane. And instead of seeing each detail and seeing it on its own level, you see the whole as a unity, and from far above.

There are many ways of having this experience, but it usually comes to you as if by chance, one fine day.

Or else you may have an experience which is almost the opposite, but amounts to the same thing. Suddenly you plunge into a depth, you move away from the things you perceived, they seem distant, superficial, unimportant; you enter an inner silence or an inner calm or an inward vision of things, a profound feeling, a more intimate perception of circumstances and things, in which all values change. And you become aware of a sort of unity, a deep identity which is one in spite of the diverse appearances.

Or else, suddenly also, the sense of limitation disappears and you enter into the perception of a kind of indefinite duration, without beginning or end, something that has always been and will always be.

These experiences come to you all at once, in a flash, for a second, a moment in your life, you do not know why or how.... There are other ways, other experiences — they are innumerable, they vary according to the person; but with this, a minute, a second of existence like that, you catch the tail of it. Then you must remember it, try to relive it, go to the depths of the experience, recall it, aspire, concentrate. This is the starting-point, the end of the guiding thread. For all who are destined to find their inner being, the truth of their being, there is always at least one moment in their life when they were no longer the same, perhaps just like a lightning-flash — but that is enough. It indicates the road you should take, it is the door that opens on this path. And so you must pass through the door, and with perseverance and an unfailing steadfastness seek to renew the state which will lead you to something more real and more total.

Many methods have been given through the ages; but a method you have been taught, a method you have read about in books or heard from a teacher, does not have the effective value of a spontaneous experience that has come for no apparent reason and is simply the blossoming of the soul's awakening, a second of contact with your psychic being which shows you the best way for you, the one most within your reach, which you will then have to follow with perseverance to reach the goal — one second which shows you how to start, the beginning.... Some get this in dreams at night, some have it at any odd time: something you see which awakens this new

consciousness in you, something you hear, a beautiful land-
scape, beautiful music, or else simply a few words you read,
or the intensity of concentration in an effort — anything at
all, there are a thousand reasons and a thousand of ways of
having it. But I repeat, all who are destined to realise have
had this at least once in their life. It may be very fleeting, it
may have been when they were very young, but always one
has, at least once in one's life, the experience of what the true
consciousness is. Well, that is the best indication of the path
to be followed.[73]

When the first experience comes, which sometimes begins when
one is very young, the first contact with the inner joy, the inner beauty, the inner light, the first contact with *that*, which
suddenly makes you feel, "Oh! that is what I want," you must
cultivate it, never forget it, hold it constantly before you, tell
yourself, "I have felt it once, so I can feel it again. It has been
real for me, if only for the space of a second, and it is what I
am going to revive in myself." . . .

This is what you should do every time you have the chance
to collect yourself, commune with yourself, seek yourself.[74]

To become conscious of anything whatever, you must will it.
And when I say "will it", I don't mean saying one day, "Oh!
I would like it very much", then two days later completely
forgetting it.

To will it is a constant, sustained, concentrated aspiration,
an almost exclusive occupation of the consciousness. This is
the first step. There are many others: a very attentive observation, a very persistent analysis, a very keen discernment of
what is pure in the movement and what is not. . . .

Each one of you should be able to get into touch with
your own psychic being, it is not an inaccessible thing. Your

psychic being is there precisely to put you in contact with the divine forces.[75]

The Decisive Change

When the consciousness feels imprisoned in its too narrow external mould, what should one do?

The Mother: Above all you must not be violent, for if you are violent you will come out of it tired, drained, without any result. You must concentrate all the forces of aspiration. If you are conscious of the inner flame, you should put into this flame all that is strongest in you by way of aspiration, of invocation, and keep as quiet as you can, calling, with a great confidence that the answer will come. And when you are in this state, with your aspiration and your concentrated force, your inner flame, press gently upon this kind of outer crust, without violence, but insistently, for as long as you can, without getting agitated, irritated or excited. You must be perfectly quiet, call and push.

It will not succeed the first time. You must begin again as many times as is necessary, but suddenly, one day… you are on the other side! Then you emerge into an ocean of light.

If you fight, if you are restless, if you struggle, you will get nothing; and if you give in to your nerves, you will just get a headache and that is all.

That is it: gather all your power of aspiration, make it something intensely concentrated in an absolute tranquillity, be conscious of your inner flame and throw into it all you can so that it may burn higher and higher, higher and higher; and then call consciously, and slowly push. You are sure to succeed one day.[76]

Concentrate in the heart. Enter into it; go within and deep

and far, as far as you can. Gather all the strings of your consciousness that are spread abroad, roll them up and take a plunge and sink down.

A fire is burning there, in the deep quietude of the heart. It is the divinity in you — your true being. Hear its voice, follow its dictates.

There are other centres of concentration, for example, one above the crown and another between the eye-brows. Each has its own efficacy and will give you a particular result. But the central being lies in the heart and from the heart proceed all central movements — all dynamism and urge for transformation and power of realisation.[77]

This change of consciousness and its preparation have often been compared to the formation of a chick in an egg: till the last second the egg remains the same, there is no change, and it is only when the chick is completely formed, absolutely alive, that it makes itself a hole in the shell with its little beak and comes out. Something similar takes place at the moment of the change of consciousness. For a long time you have the impression that nothing is happening, that your consciousness is the same as usual; and even, if you have an intense aspiration, you may feel a resistance, as though you were knocking against a wall that refuses to yield. But when you are ready within, a last effort — a peck at the shell of your being — and everything opens and you are projected into another consciousness.[78]

The Sense of Eternity

The Mother: To find the soul you must go like this (*gesture of plunging*), like this, draw back from the surface, dive deep and enter, enter, enter, go down, down, down into a deep hole, very deep, silent, immobile; and there, there is a kind of...

something warm, quiet, rich in substance and very still, very full, like a sense of sweetness — that is the soul.

And if you persist and are conscious, then there comes a kind of plenitude that gives the feeling of something complete and containing unfathomable depths in which, should you enter, you feel that many secrets would be revealed... like the reflection in very peaceful waters of something eternal. And you no longer feel limited by time.

You have the impression that you have always been and will be for eternity.

That is when you have touched the core of the soul.

And if the contact has been conscious and complete enough, it liberates you from bondage to outer forms; you no longer feel that you live only because you have a body. That is usually the normal sensation of the human being, to be so tied to this outer form that when I think of "myself" I think of the body. That is the normal thing. The reality of the person is the reality of the body. Only when one has made an effort for inner development and tried to find something a little more stable in one's being, can one begin to feel that this "something", which is permanently conscious through all ages and all change, must be "myself".[79]

Behind the whole creation (I am speaking of the material creation), there is a perfect silence, which is not the opposite of noise, but a positive silence, and it is at the same time a complete immobility. That is very good as an antidote to disorder. But the sense of eternity is still better, and has a sweetness that is not there in the other; the sense of eternity includes also the sense of sweetness (but not sweetness as we understand it). It is extremely "comfortable", that is, there is no reason why it should change or cease or start again. It is like that, it is perfect in itself. And these are the best antidotes to the other state [of disorder]: peace, simple peace, is not always enough.[80]

8

Secrets of the Body-Consciousness

Sri Aurobindo: Each plane of our being — mental, vital, physical — has its own consciousness, separate though interconnected and interacting; but to our outer mind and sense, in our waking experience, they are all confused together. The body, for instance, has its own consciousness and acts from it, even without any mental will of our own or even against that will, and our surface mind knows very little about this body-consciousness, feels it only in an imperfect way, sees only its results and has the greatest difficulty in finding out their causes. It is part of the yoga to become aware of this separate consciousness of the body, to see and feel its movements and the forces that act upon it from inside or outside and to learn how to control and direct it even in its most hidden and (to us) subconscient processes.[81]

The body is mostly unconscious or rather subconscious — it has to be made conscious.

How is one to make it conscious?

By bringing down the true consciousness into it and by being quiet, vigilant and conscious in the mind and vital.[82]

The physical sadhana is to bring down the higher light and power and peace and Ananda into the body consciousness, to get rid of the inertia of the physical, the doubts, limitations, external tendency of the physical mind, the defective energies of the vital physical (nerves) and bring in instead the true consciousness there so that the physical may be a perfect instrument for the Divine Will.[83]

Finally, the body obeys the mind automatically in those things in which it is formed or trained to obey it, but the relation of the body to the mind is not in all things that of an automatic perfect instrument. The body also has a consciousness of its own and, though it is a submental instrument or servant consciousness, it can disobey or fail to obey as well. In many things, in matters of health and illness for instance, in all automatic functionings, the body acts on its own and is not a servant of the mind. If it is fatigued, it can offer a passive resistance to the mind's will. It can cloud the mind with *tamas*, inertia, dullness, fumes of the subconscient so that the mind cannot act. The arm lifts, no doubt, when it gets the suggestion, but at first the legs do not obey when they are asked to walk; they have to learn how to leave the crawling attitude and movement and take up the erect and ambulatory habit. When you first ask the hand to draw a straight line or to play music, it can't do it and won't do it. It has to be schooled, trained, taught, and afterwards it does automatically what is required of it. All this proves that there is a body-consciousness which can do things at the mind's order, but has to be awakened, trained, made a good and conscious instrument. It can even be so trained that a mental will or suggestion can cure the illness of the body.[84]

The Mother: The most important thing in therapeutics is to teach the body to react properly and reject the illness.[85]

The body is cured if it has decided to be cured.[86]

The body has a consciousness that is quite personal to it and totally independent of the mind. The body is fully aware of its own functioning, of its own equilibrium or disequilibrium, and it becomes absolutely conscious in a very precise way if there is a disorder somewhere or other, . . . even if there are no outward symptoms. The body knows if its whole functioning is harmonious, well-balanced, well-regulated, proceeding as it should; it has this kind of plenitude — a sense of plenitude, joy and strength — something like the joy of living, acting, moving in an equilibrium full of life and energy. Or else the body can be aware that it is ill-treated by the vital and the mind and that this is harming its own balance, and it suffers from that. This may cause a complete breakdown of its equilibrium.[87]

The Body and Its Masters

The Mother: When one has developed this body-consciousness, one can have a very clear perception of the contradiction between the different kinds of consciousness. When the body needs something and knows this is what it needs, and the vital wants something else and the mind yet another thing, well, there may very well be an argument among them, contradictions and conflicts. And one can discern very well what the equilibrium of the body is, the need of the body in itself, and how the vital interferes and usually destroys this equilibrium and does so much harm to the development, because it is ignorant. And when the mind comes in, it creates yet another disorder in addition to the one between the vital and the physical, introducing its ideas, its norms, its principles, its rules, its laws and all the rest, and as it does not exactly take into account the needs of the other [the body], it wants to do what everybody else does.

Human beings have a much more delicate and uncertain health than animals because their mind intervenes and disturbs the equilibrium. The body, left to itself, has a sure instinct. For example, never will the body if left to itself eat when it doesn't need to or take something that will be harmful to it. And it will sleep when it needs to sleep, it will act when it needs to act. The instinct of the body is very sure. It is the vital and the mind which disturb it, the one by its desires and caprices, the other by its principles, dogmas, laws and ideas. And unfortunately, in civilisation as it is understood, with the kind of education given to children, this sure instinct of the body is completely destroyed: it is the rest that dominate. And naturally things happen as they do: one eats things that are harmful, one doesn't take rest when one needs to or sleeps too much when it is not necessary or does things one should not do and spoils one's health completely.[88]

The body is much less difficult to organise than the vital, for instance. But the mind and the vital, with the character and temperament they have, what don't they do to this poor slave of a body! After mistreating it, perhaps spoiling it (it protests a little, falls somewhat ill), the two accomplices say: "What a beast is this body, it cannot follow us in our movement!" Unfortunately the body obeys its masters, the mind and vital, blindly, without any discrimination. The mind comes along with its theories: "You must not eat this, it will harm you; you must not do that, it is bad", and if the mind is not wise and clear-sighted, the poor body suffers the consequences of the orders it receives. And I will not speak of the orders it receives from the vital. The mind with its rigid principles and the vital with its excesses and outbursts and passions are quick to destroy the body's equilibrium and to create a condition of fatigue, exhaustion and illness.[89]

By its very nature it [the body] is a docile and faithful servant. Unfortunately, it rarely has the capacity of discernment it ought to have with regard to its masters, the mind and the vital. It obeys them blindly, at the cost of its own well-being. . . . It must be freed from this tyranny and this can be done only through a constant union with the psychic centre of the being. The body has a wonderful capacity of adaptation and endurance. It is able to do so many more things than one usually imagines. If instead of the ignorant and despotic masters that now govern it, it is ruled by the central truth of the being, you will be amazed at what it is capable of doing.[90]

Letting the Body Restore Its Balance

The Mother: Even simply in the body, when there is something like an attack, an accident, an illness trying to attack it — something like that, an attack on the body — a body left to its natural spontaneity has an urge, an aspiration, a spontaneous will to call for help. But as soon as it enters the head, it takes the form of the things we are used to and everything is spoiled. But if you see the body in itself, as it is, there is something that suddenly wakes up and calls for help — but with such a faith, such an intensity, just as a little baby calls its mama. . . . The body left to itself, without this kind of constant action of the mind upon it, has this: as soon as something gets disturbed, immediately it has an aspiration, a call, a seeking for help, and this is very powerful. If nothing interferes, it is very powerful. It is as though the cells themselves sprang up in an aspiration, a call.

Hidden in the body are priceless unknown treasures. In all its cells there is an intensity of life, aspiration, will for progress which usually we do not even realise. The body-consciousness would have to be completely warped by the action of the mind and vital for it not to have an immediate will to re-establish its equilibrium. When this will is not there, it means that the whole body-consciousness has been spoiled by the intervention of the mind and vital. When people cherish their illness more or less subconsciously with a sort of morbidity under the pretext that it makes them interesting, it is not their body at all — poor body! — it is something they have imposed on it with a mental or vital perversion. The body, if left to itself, is remarkable, for not only does it aspire for equilibrium and well-being but it is capable of restoring its own balance. If you leave your body alone without interfering with all your thoughts, your vital reactions, your depressions, all your so-called knowledge, your mental constructions, your fears — if you leave the body to itself, spontaneously it will do what is necessary to set itself right again.

The body in its natural state likes equilibrium, likes harmony; it is the other parts of the being which spoil everything.

Mother, how can one prevent the mind from interfering?

Ah! first you must want it, and then you must... as when people make a lot of noise and one tells them, "Keep quiet, keep quiet, keep quiet!", you must do that when the mind comes along with all its suggestions and its movements. You must quiet it, pacify it, make it be silent.

The first thing is not to listen to it. Most of the time, as soon as all these thoughts come, one looks at them, tries to understand, listens, so naturally the fool thinks you are very interested and increases its activity. You must not listen, not pay attention. If it makes too much noise, you must tell it: "Be still! Now then, silence, keep quiet!" without making a lot of noise yourself, you understand. You must not do like people who start shouting, "Keep quiet", and make so much noise themselves that they are even worse than the others![91]

The Certitude of Cure

The Mother: When you are normal, that is to say, not spoiled by bad teaching and bad examples, when you are born and live in a healthy and relatively balanced and normal environment, the body, spontaneously, without any need to intervene mentally or even vitally, has the certitude that even if something goes wrong it will be cured. The body carries within itself the certitude of cure, the certitude that the illness or disorder is sure to disappear. Only through false education from the environment is the body gradually taught that there are incurable diseases, irreparable accidents, and that one grows old, and all these stupidities which undermine its faith and confidence. But normally, the body of a normal child — the body, I am not speaking of the mind — the body itself feels when something goes wrong that it will certainly be all right again. And if it is not like that, it means that it has already been perverted. It seems *normal* for it to be in good health, it seems quite abnormal to it if something goes wrong and it falls ill; and in its instinct, its spontaneous instinct, it is sure that everything will be all right. It is only the perversion of thought which destroys this; as one grows up, the thought becomes more and more distorted, there are all the collective suggestions, and so, little by little, the body loses its trust in itself, and naturally, losing its self-confidence, it also loses the spontaneous capacity of restoring its equilibrium when it has been disturbed.

But if when very young, from your earliest childhood, you have been taught all sorts of discouraging, depressing things — things that cause decomposition, so to speak, or disintegration — then this poor body does its best, but it has been perverted, corrupted, and no longer has the sense of its inner strength, its inner force, its power to react.

If you take care not to corrupt it, the body carries within itself the certitude of victory. Only the wrong use we make of thought and its influence on the body robs it of this certitude of victory. So the first thing to do is to cultivate this certitude instead of destroying it. And when it is there, no effort is needed to aspire, but simply a flowering, an unfolding of that inner certitude of victory.

The body carries within itself the sense of its divinity. This is what you must try to recover in yourself if you have lost it.[92]

You must tell a child — or yourself if you are no longer just a baby — "Everything in me that seems unreal, impossible, illusory, *that* is what is true, *that* is what I must cultivate." When you have these aspirations: "Oh, not to be limited all the time by some incapacity, held back all the time by some bad will!", you must cultivate in yourself the certitude that *that* is what is essentially true and *that* is what must be realised.

Then faith awakens in the cells of the body. And you will see that you find a response in your body itself. The body itself will feel that if its inner will helps, fortifies, directs, leads, well, all its limitations will gradually disappear.[93]

The Vibratory Process of an Illness

The Mother: I have some interesting things to tell you. It is about that cold. An extraordinary healing power... All the phases in their most acute form, with the study of the process, going through each phase in a few hours, or a few minutes (depending on what it was). When you have a cold, you usually go through one phase, then another (you know how it is), then it goes lower down, then there is a cough, then... All of it was gone through quickly, and in two days it was over. And with the whole process, but not the mentalised process, not at all: the vibratory process, showing how the Force comes and acts, and at the same time... Oh, it was very, very interesting, because there was the part played by the inconscient, the part played by conscious reactions, the part played by the will (that is tremendous, an enormous part), the part played by mental suggestion (tremendous, too), and... the action of the supreme Vibration. The whole thing in detail, day and night, constantly. . . .

Take the coughing, for instance (not in the chest, in the

throat). So, the first vibration: an irritation that draws your attention in order to make you cough. It has a certain kind of vibration which we may call "pointed", but it is not violent: it is light, annoying. It is the first little vibration. So with that vibration, awakening of the attention in the surrounding consciousness [of the throat cells]; then refusal to accept the cough, a rejection here [in the throat], which at first almost causes nausea (all this is seen through a microscope, you understand, they are tiny things). The attention is focussed. Then, at that point, there are several possible factors, sometimes simultaneous and sometimes one driving the other away; one is anxiety: something goes wrong and there is apprehension at what is going to happen; another is a will that nothing should be disturbed by the irritation; and all of a sudden, the faith that the Force is capable of restoring order everywhere instantly — none of this is intellectual: it is vibrations.

Then, sometime yesterday morning, something very interesting took place: a clear perception that the vast majority of the cells (in *this* case: I am not talking about the whole body, I am talking about this particular spot — throat, nose, etc.), that the vast majority of the cells still have a sort of feeling — which seems to be the result of innumerable experiences or of habits (it is both; not clearly one or the other, but both) — that Nature's force, that is to say, the nature governing the body, knows what needs to be done better than the divine Power: it is "used to it", it "knows it better". That is how it is. So then, when this new consciousness which is being worked out in the physical being caught hold of that, oh, it was as if it had caught hold of an extraordinary revelation; it said, "Ah, I've caught you, you are the culprit! You are the one who is preventing the transformation." . . .

And that cold came as a magnifying glass, you understand. It came and magnified everything so it would become more visible and more easily observed. And the detail of all that is going on is, oh, really marvellous: it is a whole world, and it is tiny little things that generally go unobserved because we observe mentally. . . .

All this must be going on in everyone, but people are unconscious. It is the consciousness of the cells which has awakened, you understand. It is so interesting! And how illnesses can be avoided, how things... All of it based on the experience of the *unreality of appearances*: a play is going on behind, which is altogether different from what we see or know.[94]

A Shift in Consciousness

The Mother: The experience I have been having for months now, especially since this year, that the "shift" of the consciousness... instead of the consciousness being in the ordinary state, if you shift it (I am speaking of the consciousness of the body), if it is directly tuned in to the Divine, in a few... sometimes it is seconds, sometimes it is minutes, but in a few minutes the ailment absolutely disappears. And if you just do this (*Mother slightly tilts a finger to the left*), you go backward a little, it comes back immediately. And if you keep your consciousness in the right position, it is perfect.

That is an experience I have had more than a hundred times, even with such things as a toothache, — and that is a pain difficult to cure — even sharp pains in one place or another. The experience is had *by the body*. The body knows it.

(Long silence)

It is very interesting because it is an experience had in every detail and every stage. The first thing it found was not to think of the ailment, not to be occupied with it. That is the first stage. Afterwards, it found that when it was occupied with something else, it subsided very much. Afterwards, it had the experience that if someone comes near it who knows you are ailing, it comes back! All that is very, very interesting: lots of little verifications every minute. And finally it had the repeated and absolutely convincing proof that as soon as it concentrates on the Divine, it enters into relation (because it *feels*, it has the sensation in the cells), as soon as it concentrates (without being concerned with the ailing point: it is better not to be concerned with it), it disappears totally to the point that... There are times like that (there are things that hurt, so the first effect is not to feel the pain any more), there were times in the beginning when it asked for the intervention (the body) and it had an effect, but there was the feeling of a struggle, resistance (something like that): it took a little time; but when it managed to concentrate *without demanding*, you see, simply giving oneself to the Divine, then it does not think about it, the body itself no longer thinks about the pain, but after a certain time, it sees that it is completely gone! — it wasn't thinking of it, there is no longer anything.

That experience has been repeated *hundreds* of times for all sorts of different things.[95]

I have seen it — a physical suffering that lasts, that does not stop, that lasts day and night. And then all of a sudden, instead of being in this state of consciousness, you are in that of this exclusive divine Presence. Pain gone! And it was physical, altogether physical, with a physical reason. Yes, the doctors would say, "It is because of this, because of that and that", quite a material thing, purely physical; and poof! it goes away.... The consciousness changes and back it comes.

If one remains long enough in the true consciousness, the appearance, that is to say, what we call the physical "fact" [of the illness], that itself disappears, not just the pain.[96]

The Body as the Expression of a Deeper Reality

The Mother: The cure for all physical disorders lies in the cells becoming convinced — conscious and convinced — that they are an expression of the Divine, or even that they are divine in their essence.[97]

Through repeated, daily experiences, I am convinced more and more that every disorder in the body and all illnesses are the result of *doubt* in the cells or a certain group of cells. They doubt the concrete reality of the Divine, they doubt the Divine Presence in them, they doubt that they are divine in their very essence, and this doubt is the cause of all disorders.

As soon as you succeed in infusing into them the certitude of the Divine, the disorder disappears almost instantly, and it recurs only because, not having been definitively driven away, the doubt reappears.[98]

When there is a clearly localised ailment in the body, what is the best way to open the physical consciousness to receive the healing Force?

Everyone must find his own movement; because for each person, what is most effective is the method for which he has been more or less prepared and which is most familiar to him. So it is very difficult to make a general rule.

But a preparation of a general kind is possible. This is to accustom the body methodically to understand that it is only the outer expression of a truer and deeper reality, and that this truer and deeper reality is what governs its destiny — though it is not usually aware of it.

You can prepare the body through a series of observations,... by showing it examples, making it understand things as one makes a child understand them, either by observing its own movements — but here one is usually rather blind! — or by observing those of others.... Take this, for instance: a certain number of people, placed in precisely similar circumstances, are each affected very differently. We may go even further: in a given set of definite circumstances, given a certain number of definite individuals in apparently identical conditions, for some the results are catastrophic, while others escape unharmed.

During the war there were a great many examples of this kind for study. In epidemics it is the same thing; in natural calamities, such as tidal waves, earthquakes or cyclones, it is the same.

The body understands these things if they are shown and explained to it as one explains things to a child: "You see, there was something *else* that acted there, not only the brute material fact by itself." Unless some bad will prevents it, it understands.

This is a preparation. . . .

Three Steps to Heal All Disorder

Now suppose that due to some illness or other you have some pain at a particular spot. At that moment all will depend, as I said at the beginning, on the approach most familiar to you. But we can give an example. You are in pain, in great pain; it hurts very much, you are suffering a lot.

First point: do not dwell on the pain by telling yourself, "Oh, how it hurts! Oh, this pain is unbearable! Oh, it is getting worse and worse, I will never be able to endure it", etc., all that sort of thing. The more you go on thinking like that and feeling like that and the more your attention is concentrated on it, the more the pain increases remarkably.

So, the first point: to control yourself enough not to do that.

Second point: as I said, it depends on your habits. If you know how to concentrate, to be quiet, and if you can bring into yourself a certain peace of any kind — it may be a mental peace, it may be a vital peace, it may be a psychic peace; they have different values and qualities, that is an individual question — you try to realise within yourself a state of peace or you attempt to enter into conscious contact with a force of peace.... Suppose you succeed to a greater or less extent. Then, if you can draw the peace into yourself and bring it down into the solar plexus — for we are not talking about inner states, we are talking about your physical body — and from there direct it very calmly, very slowly, so to speak, but very persistently, towards the place where the pain is more or less acute, and fix it there, this is very good.

This is not always enough.

But if by widening this movement you can add a sort of mental formation with a little life in it (not just cold, but with a little life in it) that the only reality is the divine Reality, and all the cells of this body are a more or less deformed expression of that divine Reality — there is only one reality, the Divine, and our body is a more or less deformed expression of that sole Reality — if by my aspiration, by my concentration, I can bring into the cells of the body the consciousness of that sole Reality, all disorder must necessarily cease.

If you can add to this a movement of trusting surrender to the Grace, I guarantee that within five minutes your suffering will disappear. If you know how to do it.

You may try and yet not succeed. You must know how to try again and again and again, until you do succeed. But if you do these three things at the same time, well, there is no pain that can resist.[99]

Part Three

Cure by Spiritual Force

The human body has always been in the habit of answering to whatever forces chose to lay hands on it and illness is the price it pays for its inertia and ignorance. It has to learn to answer to the one Force alone.[1]

Sri Aurobindo

1

Divine Grace

What should one do who wants to change his bodily condition, effect a cure or correct some physical imperfection? Should he concentrate upon the end to be realised and exercise his will-power or should he only live in the confidence that it will be done or trust in the Divine Power to bring about the desired result in its own time and in its own way?

The Mother: All these are so many ways of doing the same thing and each in different conditions can be effective. The method by which you will be most successful depends on the consciousness you have developed and the character of the forces you are able to bring into play. You can live in the consciousness of the completed cure or change and by the force of your inner formation slowly bring about the outward change. Or if you know and have the vision of the force that is able to effect these things and if you have the skill to handle it, you can call it down and apply it in the parts where its action is needed, and it will work out the change. Or, again, you can present your difficulty to the Divine and ask of It the cure, putting confidently your trust in the Divine Power.

But whatever you do, whatever the process you use, and even if you happen to have acquired in it a great skill and power, you must leave the result in the hands of the Divine. Always you may try, but it is for the Divine to give you the fruit of your effort or not to give it. There your personal power stops; if the result comes, it is the Divine Power and not yours that brings it. You question if it is right to ask the Divine for these things. But there is no more harm in turning to the Divine for the removal of a physical imperfection than in praying for the removal of a moral defect. But whatever you ask for or whatever your effort, you must feel, even while trying your best, using knowledge or putting forth power, that the result depends upon the Divine Grace. Once you have taken up the Yoga, whatever you do must be done in a spirit of complete surrender. This must be your attitude, — "I aspire, I try to cure my imperfections, I do my best, but for the result I put myself entirely into the hands of the Divine."

> *Does it help, if you say, "I am sure of the result, I know that the Divine will give me what I want"?*

You may take it in that way. The very intensity of your faith may mean that the Divine has already chosen that the thing it points to shall be done. An unshakable faith is a sign of the presence of the Divine Will, an evidence of what shall be.[2]

Only the Divine can heal. It is in *Him alone* that one must seek help and support, it is in *Him alone* that one must put all one's hope.[3]

Each time an illness is cured, each time an accident is avoided, each time a catastrophe, even a global one, is averted, in all these things, it is always an intervention of the vibration of harmony in the vibration of disorder that causes the disorder to cease.

So the people — the faithful — who always say, "By the grace of God, this has happened", are not so wrong.

I am simply observing a fact, that this vibration of order and harmony intervenes — the causes of its intervention are another matter, it is merely a scientific observation.[4]

Sri Aurobindo: I should like to say something about the Divine Grace — for you seem to think it should be something like a Divine Reason acting upon lines not very different from those of human intelligence. But it is not that. Also it is not a universal Divine Compassion either, acting impartially on all who approach it and acceding to all prayers. It does not select the righteous and reject the sinner. . . . It is a power that is superior to any rule, even to the Cosmic Law — for all spiritual seers have distinguished between the Law and Grace. Yet it is not indiscriminate — only it has a discrimination of its own which sees things and persons and the right times and seasons with another vision than that of the Mind or any other normal Power. A state of Grace is prepared in the individual often behind thick veils by means not calculable by the mind and when the state of Grace comes, then the Grace itself acts. There are these three powers: (1) The Cosmic Law, of Karma or what else; (2) the Divine Compassion acting on as many as it can reach through the nets of the Law and giving them their chance; (3) the Divine Grace which acts more incalculably but also more irresistibly than the others. The only question is whether there is something behind all the anomalies of life which can respond to the call and open itself with whatever difficulty till it is ready for the illumination of the Divine Grace — and that *something* must be not a mental and vital movement but an inner somewhat which can well be seen by the inner eye. If it is there and when it becomes active in front, then the Compassion can act, though the full action of the Grace may still wait attending the decisive decision or change; for this may be postponed to a future hour, because some portion or element of the being may still come between, something that is not yet ready to receive.

But why allow *anything* to come in the way between you and the Divine, any idea, any incident? When you are in full aspiration and joy, let nothing count, nothing be of any importance except the Divine and your aspiration. If one wants the Divine quickly, absolutely, entirely, that must be the spirit of approach, absolute, all-engrossing, making that the one point with which nothing else must interfere.[5]

Letting the Grace Work

The Mother: The human mind arranges and combines things, accepts or eliminates them according to its own notions and judgment. It does not leave any room for the Grace. For instance, one is cured of a disease or passes an examination; one thinks it is due to medicine or one's effort. One does not see that in between these factors or behind them there may be the Grace acting. . . .

If one does not recognise the Grace, how can it work? It is as if one had shut one's door against it. Of course, it can work from below, underneath, so to speak.

Doesn't the Grace act unconditionally?

. . . Yes, the Grace is unconditional; but at the same time how will it work if a man is throwing it away or does not recognise it? It would be like constantly spilling from a cup in which something is being poured. If one recognises the Grace and expresses gratitude, it acts more quickly and more powerfully.

Isn't it because we are ignorant that we don't recognise it?

No; I know many ignorant people who having received the Grace have expressed a deep gratitude welling up from the heart. . . .

But the Grace does not work according to human standards or demands. It has its own law and its own way. How can it act otherwise? Very often what seems to be a great blow or calamity at the present moment may turn out to be a great blessing after ten years or so, and people say that their real life began only after that mishap.[6]

The Grace is always there ready to act but you must let it

work and not resist its action. The one condition required is faith.[7]

Faith in the Divine

The Mother: All the circumstances of life are arranged to teach us that, beyond mind, faith in the Divine Grace gives us the strength to go through all trials, to overcome all weaknesses and find the contact with the Divine Consciousness which gives us not only peace and joy but also physical balance and good health.[8]

One must never lose hope or faith — there is nothing incurable, and no limit can be set to the power of the Divine.[9]

If you want my *true* way of seeing things, I must tell you that taking a good dose of faith and confidence in the Divine Grace is better than all the pills and injections in the world.[10]

I quite agree with you that there is a power other and much more powerful than that of the doctors and the medicines and I am glad to see that you put your trust in it. Surely it will lead you through all difficulties and in spite of all catastrophic warnings. Keep your faith intact and all will be all right.[11]

Finally it is Faith that cures.[12]

Psychic Faith and Integral Faith

To which plane does faith belong — mental or psychic?

The Mother: Faith is an exclusively psychic phenomenon.[13]

The perception of the exterior consciousness may deny the perception of the psychic. But the psychic has the true knowledge, an intuitive instinctive knowledge. It says, "I know; I cannot give reasons, but I know." For its knowledge is not mental, based on experience or proved true. It does not believe after proofs are given: faith is the movement of the soul whose knowledge is spontaneous and direct. Even if the whole world denies and brings forward a thousand proofs to the contrary, still it knows by an inner knowledge, a direct perception that can stand against everything, a perception by identity. The knowledge of the psychic is something which is concrete and tangible, a solid mass. You can also bring it into your mental, your vital and your physical; and then you have an integral faith — a faith which can really move mountains. But nothing in the being must come and say, "It is not like that", or ask for a test. By the least half-belief you spoil matters. How can the Supreme manifest if faith is not integral and immovable? Faith in itself is always unshakable — that is its very nature, for otherwise it is not faith at all. But it may happen that the mind or the vital or the physical does not follow the psychic movement. . . . You will always miss your destiny if you start arguing. Some people sit down and con- sider whether the psychic impulse is reasonable or not.

It is not really by what is called blind faith that people are misled. . . . Pure in itself, faith can get mixed up in the being with low movements and it is then that you are misled.[14]

Faith and Effort

Sri Aurobindo: Faith can be tamasic and ineffective, e.g. "I believe the Mother will do everything, so I will do nothing. When she wants, she will transform me." That is not a dynamic but a static and inert faith.[15]

The Mother: A pure faith is something all-powerful and irresistible. One doesn't often find a faith that is all-powerful and irresistible, and this shows that it is not quite pure. The question should be put like this: each one of us has a faith, for example, a faith in something, say a faith in the divine Presence within us. If our faith were pure, we would at once be aware of this divine Presence within us. This example is very easy to understand. You have faith, it is there, but you don't have the experience. Why? Because the faith is not pure. If the faith were quite pure, immediately, the thing would be done. This is very true. So, when you become aware that the thing is not realised at once, you can begin to look: "But why isn't it realised? What is there in my faith?"[16]

Certainly a personal effort is needed to preserve one's faith, to let it grow within. Later — much later — one day, looking back, we may see that everything that happened, even what seemed to us the worst, was a divine Grace to make us advance on the way; and then we become aware that the personal effort too was a grace. But before reaching that point, one has to advance much, to struggle much, sometimes even to suffer a great deal.

To sit down in inert passivity and say, "If I am to have faith I shall have it, the Divine will give it to me", is an attitude of laziness, of unconsciousness and almost of bad-will. For the inner flame to burn, one must feed it; one must watch over the fire, throw into it the fuel of all the errors one wants to get rid of, all that delays the progress, all that darkens the path. If one doesn't feed the fire, it smoulders under the ashes of one's unconsciousness and inertia, and then, not years but lives, centuries will pass before one reaches the goal.

One must watch over one's faith as one watches over the birth of something *infinitely* precious, and protect it very carefully from everything that can impair it.

In the ignorance and darkness of the beginning, faith is the most direct expression of the Divine Power which comes to fight and conquer.[17]

Miracles of the Grace

The Mother: To fix rigid laws in this way... cuts you off from the curative Power of the Spirit, it cuts you off from the true Power of the Grace, for you can understand that if by your aspiration or your attitude you introduce a higher element, a new element — what we may now call a supramental element — into the existing combinations, you can suddenly change their nature, and all these so-called necessary and ineluctable laws become absurdities. That is to say that you yourself, with your conception, with your attitude and your acceptance of certain alleged principles, you yourself close the door upon the possibility of the miracle — they are not miracles when one knows how they happen, but obviously for the outer consciousness they seem miraculous. And it is you *yourself*, saying to yourself with a logic that seems quite reasonable, "Well, if I do this, that will necessarily happen, or if I don't do that, necessarily this other thing will happen", it is you yourself who close the door — it is as though you were putting an iron curtain between yourself and the free action of the Grace.[18]

We must learn to rely only on the Divine Grace and to call for its help in all circumstances; then it will work out constant miracles.[19]

Nothing is inevitable. At every moment an intervention may come from a higher plane into the material one and alter the course of circumstances. But in this particular case there is a conflict between a very powerful mental construction founded on medical opinion and your faith in the divine Grace.

The power of this medical suggestion lies in the fact that it insinuates itself into the subconscious and acts on the body from there, undetected even by the conscious mind unless it is in the habit of scouring the subconscious with the vigilance of a detective.

So there we are — I cannot promise you that your faith in the Grace will be intense and unshakable enough to overcome the harmful effect of these medical suggestions; and I feel that I have no right to tell you, "It is nothing," when everything in your material consciousness is crying out, "Danger!"

Rest assured that our help and our blessings are always with you.[20]

Divine Intervention

Sri Aurobindo: The Divine Grace is there ready to act at every moment, but it manifests as one grows out of the Law of Ignorance into the Law of Light, and it is meant, not as an arbitrary caprice, however miraculous often its intervention, but as a help in that growth and a Light that leads and eventually delivers.[21]

This divine grace . . . is not simply a mysterious flow or touch coming from above, but the all-pervading act of a divine presence which we come to know within as the power of the highest Self and Master of our being entering into the soul and so possessing it that we not only feel it close to us and pressing upon our mortal nature, but live in its law, know that law, possess it as the whole power of our spiritualised nature.[22]

The Mother: No matter how great your faith and trust in the divine Grace, no matter how great your capacity to see it at work in all circumstances, at every moment, at every point in life, you will never succeed in understanding the marvellous immensity of Its Action, and the precision, the exactitude with which this Action is accomplished; you will never be able to grasp to what extent the Grace does everything, is behind everything, organises everything, conducts everything, so that the march forward to the divine realisation may be as swift, as complete, as total and harmonious as possible, considering the circumstances of the world.

As soon as you are in contact with It there is not a second in time, not a point in space, which does not show you *dazzlingly* this perpetual work of the Grace, this constant intervention of the Grace.

And once you have seen this, you feel you are never equal to it, for you should never forget it, never have any fears, any anguish, any regrets, any recoils... or even suffering. If one were in union with this Grace, if one saw It everywhere, one would begin living a life of exultation, of all-power, of infinite happiness. And that would be the best possible collaboration in the divine Work.[23]

In the whole manifestation there is an infinite Grace constantly at work to bring the world out of the misery, the obscurity and the stupidity in which it lies. From all time this Grace has been at work, unremitting in its effort, and how many thousands of years were necessary for this world to awaken to the need for something greater, more true, more beautiful.

Everyone can gauge, from the resistance he meets in his own being, the tremendous resistance which the world opposes to the work of the Grace.

And it is only when one understands that *all* external things, all mental constructions, all material efforts are vain, futile, if they are not entirely consecrated to this Light and Force from above, to this Truth which is trying to express itself, that one is ready to make decisive progress. So the only truly effective attitude is a perfect, total, fervent giving of our being to That which is above us and which alone has the power to change everything.

When you open to the Spirit within you it brings you a first foretaste of that higher life which alone is worth living, then comes the will to rise to that, the hope of reaching it, the certitude that this is possible, and finally the strength to make the necessary effort and the resolution to go to the very end.

First one must wake up, then one can conquer.[24]

2

Spiritual Force

Sri Aurobindo: There is a force which accompanies the growth of the new consciousness and at once grows with it and helps it to come about and to perfect itself. This force is the Yoga-Shakti. It is here coiled up and asleep in all the centres of our inner being (Chakras) and is at the base what is called in the Tantras the Kundalini Shakti. But it is also above us, above our head as the Divine Force — not there coiled up, involved, asleep, but awake, scient, potent, extended and wide; it is there waiting for manifestation and to this Force we have to open ourselves — to the power of the Mother.[25]

What is the Yogic method of getting rid of a pain or illness?

To separate yourself from the thing and call in the Mother's Force to cure it — or else to use your will force with faith in the power to heal, having the support of the Mother's Force behind you. If you cannot use either of these methods then you must rely on the action of the medicines.[26]

All life is the play of universal forces. The individual gives a personal form to these universal forces. But he can choose whether he shall respond or not to the action of a particular force. Only most people do not really choose — they indulge the play of the forces. Your illnesses, depressions etc. are the repeated play of such forces. It is only when one can make oneself free of them that one can be the true person and have a true life — but one can be free only by living in the Divine.[27]

The Efficacy of the Force for Cure

Sri Aurobindo: It is evident that if spiritual force exists, it must be able to produce spiritual results. . . . Further, if it be true that spiritual force is the original one and the others are derivative from it, then there is no irrationality in supposing that spiritual force can produce mental results, vital results, physical results. It may act through mental, vital or physical energies and through the means which these energies use, or it may act directly on mind, life or Matter as the field of its own special and immediate action. Either way is *prima facie* possible. In a case of cure of illness, someone is ill for two days, weak, suffering from pains and fever; he takes no medicine, but finally asks for cure from his Guru; the next morning he rises well, strong and energetic. He has at least some justification for thinking that a force has been used on him and put into him and that it was a spiritual power that acted. . . .

It does not follow that a spiritual force must either succeed in all cases or, if it does not, that proves its non-existence. Of no force can that be said. The force of fire is to burn, but there are things it does not burn; under certain circumstances it does not burn even the feet of a man who walks barefoot on red-hot coals. That does not prove that fire cannot burn or that there is no such thing as force of fire, Agni Shakti.[28]

What about the instances where the Divine Force has failed, and why does it succeed in some cases and not in others?

The mistake is to think that it must be either a miraculous force or else none. There is no miraculous force and I do not deal in miracles. The word Divine here is out of place, if it is taken as an always omnipotently acting Power. Yogic Force is then better; it simply means a higher Consciousness using its power, a spiritual and supraphysical force acting on the physical world directly. One has to train the instrument to be a channel of this force; it works also according to a certain law and under certain conditions. The Divine does not work arbitrarily or as a thaumaturge; He acts upon the world along the lines that have been fixed by the nature and purpose of the world we live in — by an increasing action of the thing that has to manifest, not by a sudden change or disregard of all the conditions of the work to be done. If it were not so, there would be no need of Yoga or time or human action or instruments or of a Master and disciples or of a Descent or anything else. It could simply be a matter for the *tathāstu* ["so be it"] and nothing more. But that would be irrational if you like and worse than irrational — "childish". This does not mean that interventions, things apparently miraculous, do not happen — they do. But all cannot be like that. . . .

If it depended on a few cases of illness, it would be a thing of no certitude or importance. If the "Force" were a mere freak or miracle, it would be equally trivial and unimportant, even if well-attested. It is only of importance if it is part of the consciousness and the life, used at all times, not only for illness but for whatever one has to do. It manifests in various ways — as a strength of the consciousness evenly supporting the life and action, as a power put forth for this or that object of the outward life, as a special Force from above drawn down to raise and increase the scope of the consciousness and its height and transform it not by a miraculous, but by a serious, steady, organised action following certain definite lines. Its effectiveness as well as its action is determined first by its own height and intensity or that of the plane from which it comes (it may be from any plane ranging from the Higher Mind upward to the Overmind), partly by the condition of the objects or the field in which it acts, partly by the movement which it has to effect, general or particular. It is neither a magician's wand nor a child's bauble, but something one has to observe, understand, develop, master before one can use it aright or else — for few can use it except in a limited manner — be its instrument.[29]

Becoming Conscious of the Force

The Mother: There are many people who are not even conscious, the immense majority of people are not even conscious of the action of the divine Force in them. If you speak to them about it, they look at you in round-eyed wonder, they think you are half mad, they do not know what you are talking about. That is the vast majority of human beings. And yet the Consciousness is at work, working all the time. It moulds them from within whether they want it or not. But then, when they become conscious of this, there are people who are shocked by it, who are so stupid as to revolt and say: "Ah! no, I want it to be *myself*!" Myself, that is, an imbecile who knows nothing. And then, that stage too passes. At last there comes a moment when one collaborates and says: "Oh! What joy!" And you give yourself, you want to be as passive and receptive as possible so as not to stand in the way of this divine Will, this divine Consciousness that is acting. You become more and more attentive, and more sincere, you feel in what direction, in what movement this divine Consciousness is working, and you give yourself to it wholly. . . .

How should one practise this consciousness?

You must establish this will to be conscious constantly and then change the mental will into an aspiration. You must have this movement. And then never to forget. You must look, look at yourself, and look at your life with the sincerity not to make a mistake, never to deceive yourself. Oh! how difficult it is![30]

Sri Aurobindo: When I speak of feeling Force or Power, I do not mean simply having a vague sense of it, but feeling it concretely and consequently being able to direct it, manipulate it, watch its movements, be conscious of its mass and intensity and in the same way of that of other, perhaps opposing forces; all these things are possible and usual by the development of yoga.

It is not, unless it is supramental Force, a Power that acts without conditions and limits. The conditions and limits under which yoga or sadhana has to be worked out are not arbitrary or capricious; they arise from the nature of things. These including the will, receptivity, assent, self-opening and surrender of the sadhak have to be respected by the yoga-force, unless it receives a sanction from the Supreme to override everything and get something done, but that sanction is sparingly given. . . .

Still the yoga-force is always tangible and concrete in the way I have described and has tangible results. But it is invisible — not like a blow given or the rush of a motor car knocking somebody down which the physical senses can at once perceive. How is the mere physical mind to know that it is there and working? By its results? But how can it know that the results were that of the yogic force and not of something else? One of two things it must be. Either it must allow the consciousness to go inside, to become aware of inner things, to believe in the experience of the invisible and the supraphysical, and then by experience, by the opening of new capacities, it becomes conscious of these forces and can see, follow and use their workings, just as the Scientist uses the unseen forces of Nature. Or one must have faith and watch and open oneself and then it will begin to see how things happen, it will notice that when the Force was called in, there began after a time to be a result, then repetitions, more repetitions, more clear and tangible results, increasing frequency, increasing consistency of results, a feeling and awareness of the Force at work — until the experience becomes daily, regular, normal, complete. These are the two main methods, one internal, working from in outward, the other external, working from outside and calling the inner force out till it penetrates and is visible in the exterior consciousness. But neither can be done if one insists always on the extrovert attitude, the external concrete only and refuses to join to it the internal concrete — or if the physical mind at every step raises a dance of doubts which refuses to allow the nascent experience to develop. Even the Scientist carrying on a new experiment would never succeed if he allowed his mind to behave in that way.[31]

This weight or pressure on the head is always the sign that the Mother's Force is in contact with you and pressing from above to envelop your being and enter the *ādhāra* and pervade it; — usually passing by degrees through the centres on its way downward. Sometimes it comes first as Peace, sometimes as Force, sometimes as the Mother's consciousness and her presence, sometimes as Ananda.

 . . . Of course, the pressure need not always be there; but if things take the ordinary course, it usually recurs or else continues until the *ādhāra* is open and there is no further obstacle to the descent of the higher consciousness.[32]

3

Receptivity and Resistance to the Force

You have said that on the material plane "receptivity is mixed with a large amount of resistance."[33] *What is this resistance?*

The Mother: You don't have resistances in your body? When you want to do an exercise, can you do with your body whatever you want? And when you try to be in good health, does your body always obey? . . . That is the resistance, it is all that refuses to progress. And I believe that unfortunately the amount of resistance is much greater than the amount of receptivity. One must work very hard to become receptive.

. . . You cannot imagine the immense flood of force at your disposal! And generally you do not feel it even. When you feel it, something in you shrinks because it is too much and produces a kind of instinctive fear in your cells; and when you receive it, more than three quarters of it you throw away like an overfilled vessel! It gushes out, spills over, because you are not able to hold it. I have met a very large number of people who complained that they were receiving nothing, that is to say, they said they did not have the forces they needed. It was because they were absolutely incapable of receiving them, and there was a hundred thousand times more force than what they could receive. It is like that. You are all in a sea of tremendous vibrations, and you are not at all aware of it because you are not receptive. . . . But if one were open and simply breathed in — nothing more, if one did that only — one would breathe in the Consciousness, the Light, the Understanding, the Force, the Love and all the rest. And all that is wasted upon Earth because the Earth is not ready to take it.[34]

Illness comes of resistance. You must learn to receive and hold and not resist the power of the higher Nature which is working here. The higher Nature has its own way of developing and, if you learn to keep up with it, many new splendours will open before you and, instead of illness, you will experience just the contrary. . . .

Do not resist the power for transformation and you will never fall ill.[35]

Quietude and Receptivity

The Mother: To keep quiet and concentrate, leaving the Force from above to do its work is the surest way to be cured of anything and everything. There is no illness that can resist that if it is done properly, in time and long enough, with a steady faith and a strong will.[36]

However bad your condition may be, call the light from above. Try to feel that the light is entering into you from the crown of your head bringing with it calm and peace. If you do it seriously, your headache and giddiness will disappear in no time.[37]

Sri Aurobindo: Silence is always good; but I do not mean by quietness of mind entire silence. I mean a mind free from disturbance and trouble, steady, light and glad so as to open to the Force that will change the nature. The important thing is to get rid of the habit of the invasion of troubling thoughts, wrong feelings, confusion of ideas, unhappy movements. These disturb the nature and cloud it and make it difficult for the Force to work; when the mind is quiet and at peace, the Force can work more easily.[38]

It is quite true that, left to yourself, you can do nothing; that is why you have to be in contact with the Force which is there to do for you what you cannot do for yourself. The only thing *you* have to do is to allow the force to act and put yourself on its side, which means to have faith in it, to rely upon it, not to trouble and harass yourself, to remember it quietly, to call upon it quietly, to let it act quietly.[39]

You must always try to keep the quietude, not allow depressing or disturbing thoughts or feelings to enter you or take hold of your mind or your speech. . . . If the mind keeps its quietude and receptivity to higher forces only, it can then easily pass on that quietude and receptivity to the body consciousness and even to the material cells of the body.[40]

The way in which the pains went shows you how to deal with the whole nature, — for it is the same with the mental and vital as with the physical causes of ill-ease and disturbance. To remain quiet within, to hold on to the faith and experience that to be quiet and open and let the Force work is the one way. Naturally, to be wholly conscious is not possible yet, but to feel it, to open, to let it work, to observe its results, that is the first thing. It is the beginning of consciousness and the way to complete consciousness.[41]

Increasing the Physical Receptivity

How can one increase the receptivity of the body?

The Mother: It depends on the part. The method is almost the same for all parts of the being. To begin with, the first condition: to remain as quiet as possible. You may notice that in the different parts of your being, when something comes and you do not receive it, this produces a shrinking — there is something which hardens in the vital, the mind or the body. There is a stiffening and this hurts, one feels a mental, vital or physical pain. So, the first thing is to put one's will and relax this shrinking, as one does a twitching nerve or a cramped muscle; you must learn how to relax, be able to relieve this tension in whatever part of the being it may be. The method of relaxing the contraction may be different in the mind, the vital or the body, but logically it is the same thing.

Once you have relaxed the tension, you see first if the disagreeable effect ceases, which would prove that it was a small momentary resistance, but if the pain continues and if it is indeed necessary to increase the receptivity in order to be able to receive what is helpful, what should be received, you must, after having relaxed this contraction, begin trying to widen yourself — you feel you are widening yourself. There are many methods. Some find it very useful to imagine they are floating on water with a plank under their back. Then they widen themselves, widen, until they become the vast liquid mass. Others make an effort to identify themselves with the sky and the stars, so they widen, widen themselves, identifying themselves more and more with the sky. Others again don't need these pictures; they can become conscious of their consciousness, enlarge their consciousness more and more until it becomes unlimited. One can enlarge it till it becomes as vast as the earth and even the universe. When one does that one becomes really receptive. As I have said, it is a question of training.

In any case, from an immediate point of view, when something comes and one feels that it is too strong, that it gives a headache, that one can't bear it, the method is just the same, one must act upon the contraction. One can act through thought, by calling peace, tranquillity (the feeling of peace takes away much of the difficulty) like this: "Peace, peace, peace... tranquillity... calm." Many discomforts, even physical, like all these contractions of the solar plexus, which are so unpleasant and sometimes give you nausea, the sensation of being suffocated, of not being able to recover your breath, can disappear in this way. It is the nervous centre which is affected, it gets affected very easily. As soon as there is something which affects the solar plexus, you must say, "Calm... calm... calm", become more and more calm until the tension is destroyed.[42]

Applying the Force from Outside the Body

The Mother: Take an example which is quite concrete: sunstroke. This upsets you considerably, it is one of the things which makes you most ill — a sunstroke upsets everything, it disturbs the inner functions, it generally causes a congestion in the head and very high fever. So, if this has happened, if it has succeeded in getting through the protection and entering you, well, if you can just go to a quiet place, stretch yourself out flat, go out of your body (naturally, you must learn this; there are people who do this spontaneously, for others a long discipline is necessary), go out of your body, remain above in such a way as to be able to see the body (you know the phenomenon, seeing one's body when one is outside? this can be done at will, going out of one's body and remaining just above it), the body is stretched out on a bed, a bench, on the ground, anywhere; you are stretched just above it and from there, consciously, you pull the Force from above, and if you are used to doing it, if your aspiration is strong enough, you get the answer; and then, from there, taking care not to re-enter your body, you begin to push these forces into the body, like this, regularly, until you see the body receiving them (for the first few moments they don't enter, because the body is quite upset by the illness, it is not receptive, it is curled up), you push them gently, gently, quietly, without nervousness, very peacefully, into the body. But you must not be disturbed by anyone. If someone comes along, sees you stretched out and shakes you, it is extremely dangerous. You must do this in quiet conditions, ask people not to disturb you or better shut yourself up where they can't disturb you. But you can concentrate slowly (this takes more or less time — ten minutes, half an hour, one hour, two hours — it depends upon the seriousness of the disorder which has set in), slowly, from above, you concentrate the Force until you see that the body is receiving, that the Force is entering, the disorder is being set right and there is a relaxation in the body itself. Once that is done you can get back and you are cured. This has been done for a sunstroke, which is a fairly violent thing, and also for typhoid fever, and many other illnesses. . . . Consequently, when I say that if one masters the spiritual force and knows how to use it, there is no malady which cannot be cured, I don't say it just like that in the air; it is said from experience with these things. Of course, you will say you don't know how to go out of the body, draw the Force, concentrate, have all this mastery.... It is not very common, but it is not impossible. And you can be sure that if you are helped... In fact, there is a much easier method, it is to call for help.

But the condition in every case — in every case — whether you do it yourself and depending only on yourself or whether you do it by asking someone to do it for you, the first condition: not to fear and to be calm. If you start to seethe and get fidgety in your body, it is finished, you can do nothing.

For everything — to live the spiritual life, to heal illness — for everything, one must be calm.[43]

4

Opening the Body-Consciousness

Sri Aurobindo: The physical nature is a thing of habits; it is out of habit that it responds to the forces of illness; one has to get into it the contrary habit of responding to the Divine Force only.[44]

For the Mother's Force to work fully in the body, the body itself and not only the mind must have faith and open.[45]

It is always the right inner poise, quietude inward and outward, faith, the opening of the body consciousness to the Mother and her Force that are the true means of recovery — other things can only be minor aids and devices.[46]

The body, naturally [experiences physical pain] — but the body transmits it to the vital and mental. With the ordinary consciousness the vital gets disturbed and afflicted and its forces diminished, the mind identifies and is upset. The mind has to remain unmoved, the vital unaffected, and the body has to learn to take it with equality so that the higher Force may work.[47]

It is a great gain if you feel no depression when the attack on the body comes.

The pain itself is, from your description, evidently nervous and, if you develop openness in the more physical layers of the being, then the action of the Force can always remove it or you will yourself be able to use the Force to push it away. It is a matter of getting the habit of opening in the body consciousness.[48]

The only thing to do here is to get the physical consciousness — down to the most material parts — open to the Power, then to make it accustomed to respond and obey and to each physical difficulty as it arises, apply or call in the Divine Power to throw out the attacking force.[49]

As the body consciousness becomes more open to the Force (it is always the most difficult and the last to open up entirely), this frequent stress of illness will diminish and disappear.[50]

Passivity and Inertia

Many people mistake passivity for inertia. I mistook it for a long time. I used to remain passive when I got an illness and then I found that I was consenting to it.

Sri Aurobindo: Real passivity is openness to the Higher Force; it is not inertia.[51]

It is only an inner passivity to what comes from above that is needed — inert passivity is the wrong kind of passivity.[52]

The Mother: Passivity is not laziness. An active movement is one in which you throw your force out, that is, when something comes out from you — in a movement, a thought, a feeling — something which goes out from you to others or into the world. Passivity is when you remain just yourself like this, open, and receive what comes from outside. It does not at all depend on whether one moves or sits still. It is not that at all. To be active is to throw out the consciousness or force or movement from within outwards. To be passive is to remain immobile and receive what comes from outside. . . .

You remain as though you were quite still, but open, and wait for the Force to enter, and then open yourself as wide as possible to take in all that comes into you. And it is this movement: instead of out-going vibrations there is a kind of calm quietude, but completely open, as though you were opening all your doors in this way to the force which must descend into you and transform your action and consciousness.

Receptivity is the result of a true passivity.

But Mother, to be able to become passive an effort has to be made, hasn't it?

Not necessarily, that depends upon the person. An effort? One must, yes, one must want it. But is the will an effort?... Naturally, one must think about it, must want it. But two things can go together, you see, there is a moment when the two — aspiration and passivity — can not only be alternate but simultaneous. You can be at once in the state of aspiration, of willing, which calls down something — precisely the will to open oneself and receive and the aspiration which calls down the force you want to receive — and *at the same time* be in that state of complete inner stillness which allows full penetration, for it is in this immobility that one can be penetrated, that one becomes permeable by the Force. Well, the two can be simultaneous without the one disturbing the other, or can alternate so closely that they can hardly be distinguished. But one can be like that, like a great flame rising in aspiration, and at the same time as though this flame formed a vase, a large vase, opening and receiving all that comes down.

And the two can go together. And when one succeeds in having the two together, one can have them constantly, whatever one may be doing. Only there may be a slight, very slight displacement of consciousness, almost imperceptible, which becomes aware of the flame first and then of the vase of receptivity — of what seeks to be filled and the flame that rises to call down what must fill the vase — a very slight pendular movement and so close that it gives the impression that one has the two at the same time.

(Silence)

This is one of the things one discovers gradually as the body becomes ready for transformation. It is quite a remarkable instrument in the sense that it can experience two contraries at the same time. There is a certain state of body-consciousness which brings things together, totalises things that in other states of consciousness alternate or even in certain others oppose each other. But if one has reached up there, in the vital and the mind, a development sufficient for harmonising opposites (that of course, is quite indispensable), when one has succeeded in doing this, there are moments when it alternates, you see, one thing comes after the other, while what is remarkable in the consciousness of the body is that it can feel . . . all things simultaneously, as though you were hot and cold at once, as though you were active and passive at once, and everything becomes like that. Then you begin to grasp the totality of movements in the cells. It is something much more concrete naturally, but much more perfect in the body than in any other part of the being. This means that if things continue in this way, it will be proved that the physical, material instrument is the most perfect of all. That is why perhaps it is the most difficult to transform, to perfect. But of all, it is the one most capable of perfection.[53]

Overcoming the Subconscient Resistance

Sri Aurobindo: There is no delusion about the force working in the body, but there are evidently points where there is still much resistance. The body consciousness has many parts and many different movements and these do not open or change together. Also the body is very dependent on the subconscient which has to be cleared and illumined before the body can be free from adverse reactions.[54]

The attitude of his physical mind prevents any result — for it is so unwilling to recognize anything as the result of the Force and his subconscient works in the direction of preventing any result coming — and it is the subconscient that is most determinative in matters of illness.[55]

The illness has no doubt a physical cause but there is associated with it a strong resistance to the Force which is evidently seated in the subconscient, since you are not aware of it. This is shown by the fact that after Mother put a concentrated force there yesterday, the whole thing returned more violently after an hour's relief. That is always a sign of violent and obstinate resistance somewhere. It is only if this is overcome or disappears that complete relief can come.[56]

Occasionally does it not happen that the pain or illness becomes all the more violent because the force is put on it to throw it out?

It may for a time, but if the force is strong, quiet and persistent, it will get the better of the resistance — unless something in the consciousness supports the illness or is open too much to the adverse Forces, for in that case the struggle may be a long one.[57]

The Mother: We shall have made a great leap towards realisation when we have driven all defeatism out of our consciousness.

It is by perfecting our faith in the Divine Grace that we shall be able to conquer the defeatism of the subconscient.[58]

The big difficulty in Matter is that the material consciousness (that is to say, the mind in Matter) has been formed under the pressure of difficulties — difficulties, obstacles, sufferings, struggles. It has been, so to say, "worked out" by these things and that has left upon it a stamp, almost of pessimism, defeatism, which is certainly the greatest obstacle.

It is this that I am conscious of in my own work. The most material consciousness, the most material mind is accustomed to act, to make an effort, to advance through whippings; otherwise, it is *tamas*. And then, so far as it imagines, it imagines always difficulty, always the obstacle or always the opposition, and that slows down the movement terribly. Very concrete, very tangible and *often repeated* experiences are needed to convince it that behind all its difficulties there is a Grace, behind all its failures there is the Victory, behind all its pains, its sufferings, its contradictions, there is Ananda.[59]

The Need for Perseverance

The Mother: One can succeed in pulling oneself out, so to say, from the disease, in withdrawing from it, in cutting off the relation one had with it; and then suddenly one emerges above this feeling of unease, disorder and confusion and real-

ises that one is cured. But sometimes it is enough even to remember, a movement of surprise is enough, a memory of what
it was is enough for everything to be reversed once more and
for one to have to begin the same work over again. Sometimes one has to begin again thrice, four times, ten times,
twenty times. And then some people can make the effort once,
but the second time they no longer do it well, and the third
time they don't do it at all; and they tell you, "Oh! one cannot
be cured by occult means, the divine Force doesn't cure you, it
is better to take medicines." So for these, it is better to go to
the doctor because this means that they have no spiritual perseverance and only material means can convince them of their
effectiveness.

When one wants to change something of the material life,
whether the character or the functioning of the organs or habits, one must have an unfaltering perseverance, be ready to
begin again a hundred times the same thing with the same
intensity with which one did it the first time and as though
one had never done it before.[60]

How many times during a suffering, for example, when a suffering is there, acute, and one has the impression that it is
going to become unbearable, there is the little inner movement (within the cells) of Call — the cells send their S.O.S. —
everything stops, the suffering disappeared, and often (now
more and more) it is replaced by a feeling of blissful well-
being; but the very first reaction of this imbecile material consciousness is: "Ah! we shall see how long that is going to last",
and naturally, by this movement it demolishes everything —
one must begin all over again.

I believe that for the effect to be lasting — not a miraculous effect that comes, dazzles and goes away — it must really
be the result of a *transformation*. One must be very, very patient — we have to deal with a consciousness which is very
slow, very heavy, very obstinate, which is not able to advance

rapidly, which clings to what it has, to what has appeared to it as truth; even if it is quite a tiny truth, it clings to that and does not want to move. Then to cure that, one must have very much patience — much patience.[61]

5

The Call and the Response

Sri Aurobindo: It is not a theory but a constant experience and very tangible when it comes that there is above us, above the consciousness in the physical body, a great supporting extension as it were of peace, light, power, joy — that we can become aware of it and bring it down into the physical consciousness and that that, at first for a time, afterwards more frequently and for a longer time, in the end for good, can remain and change the whole basis of our daily consciousness. Even before we are aware of it above, we can suddenly feel it coming down and entering into us. The need is to have an aspiration towards it, make the mind quiet so that what we call the opening is rendered possible.[62]

In this yoga the whole principle is to open oneself to the Divine Influence. It is there above you and, if you can once become conscious of it, you have then to call it down into you. It descends into the mind and into the body as Peace, as a Light, as a Force that works, as the Presence of the Divine with or without form, as Ananda. Before one has this consciousness, one has to have faith and aspire for the opening. Aspiration, call, prayer are forms of one and the same thing and are all effective; you can take the form that comes to you or is easiest to you.[63]

Does the intervention of the Grace come through a call?

The Mother: . . . Certainly, yes, if one has faith in the Grace and an aspiration and if one does what a little child would when it runs to its mother and says: "Mamma, give me this", if one calls with that simplicity. . . . Unless one asks for something that is not good for one, then it does not listen.[64]

When one is caught in an illness, how should one pray to the Mother?

Cure me, O Mother![65]

What is the exact way of feeling that we belong to the Divine and that the Divine is acting in us?

You must not feel with your head (because you may think so, but that is something vague); you must feel with your sense-feeling. Naturally one begins by wanting it with the mind, because that is the first thing that understands. And then one has an aspiration here (*pointing to the heart*), with a flame which pushes you to realise it. But if you want it to be truly *the* thing, well, you must sense it. . . .

How can we reach that state?

Aspire for it, want it. Try to be less and less selfish, but not in the sense of becoming nice to other people or forgetting yourself, not that: have less and less the feeling that you are a person, a separate entity, something existing in itself, isolated from the rest.

And then, above all, above all, it is that inner flame, that aspiration, that need for the light. It is a kind of — how to put it? — luminous enthusiasm that seizes you. It is an irresistible need to melt away, to give oneself, to exist only in the Divine.

At that moment you have the experience of your aspiration.

But that moment should be absolutely sincere and as integral as possible; and all this must occur not only in the head, not only here, but must take place everywhere, in all the cells of the body. The consciousness integrally must have this irresistible need.... It lasts for some time, then diminishes, gets extinguished. You cannot keep these things for very long. But then it so happens that a moment later or the next day or some time later, suddenly you have the opposite experience. Instead of feeling this ascent, all that is no longer there and you have the feeling of the Descent, the Answer. And nothing but the Answer exists.[66]

The Secret of Effective Prayer

The Mother: To aspire is indispensable. But some people aspire with such a conflict inside them between faith and absence of faith, trust and distrust, between the optimism which is sure of victory and a pessimism which asks itself when the catastrophe will come. Now if this is in the being, you may aspire but you don't get anything. And you say, "I aspired but didn't get anything." It is because you demolish your aspiration all the time by your lack of confidence. But if you truly have trust... Children when left to themselves and not deformed by older people have such a great trust that all will be well! For example, when they have a small accident, they never think that this is going to be something serious: they are spontaneously convinced that it will soon be over, and this helps so powerfully in putting an end to it.

Well, when one aspires for the Force, when one asks the Divine for help, if one asks with the unshakable certitude that it will come, that it is impossible that it won't, then it is sure to come. . . . And some people are constantly in this state. When there is something to be received, they are always there to receive it. There are others, when there is something to have, force descends, they are always absent, they are always closed at that moment; while those who have this childlike trust are always there at the right time.

And it is strange, isn't it, outwardly there is no difference. They may have exactly the same goodwill, the same aspiration, the same wish to do good, but those who have this smiling confidence within them, do not question, do not ask themselves whether they will have it or not have it, whether the Divine will answer or not — the question does not arise, it is something understood... "What I need will be given to me; if I pray I shall have an answer; if I am in a difficulty and ask for help, the help will come — and not only will it come but it will arrange everything." If the trust is there, spontaneous, candid, unquestioning, it works better than anything else, and the results are marvellous. It is with the contradictions and doubts of the mind that one spoils everything, with this kind of notion which comes when one is in difficulties: "Oh, it is impossible! I shall never manage it. And if it is going to be aggravated, if this condition I am in, which I don't want, is going to grow still worse, if I continue to slide down farther and farther, if, if, if, if..." — like that, and one builds a wall between oneself and the force one wants to receive. The psychic being has this trust, has it wonderfully, without a shadow, without an argument, without a contradiction. And when it is like that, there is not a prayer which does not get an answer, no aspiration which is not realised.[67]

When one aspires for something, if at the same time one knows that the aspiration will be heard and answered in the best way possible, that establishes a quietude in the being, a quietude in its vibrations; whilst if there is a doubt, an uncertainty, if one does not know what will lead one to the goal or if ever one will reach it or whether there is a way of doing so, and so on, then one gets disturbed and that usually creates a sort of little whirlwind around the being, which prevents it from receiving the real thing. Instead, if one has a quiet faith, if whilst aspiring one knows that there is no aspiration (naturally, sincere aspiration) which remains unanswered, then one is quiet. One aspires with as much fervour as possible, but does not stand in nervous agitation asking oneself why one does not get immediately what one has asked for. . . . To be very quiet, calm, peaceful, with the faith that what is true will take place, and that if one lets it happen, it will happen so much faster. Then, in that peace everything goes much better.[68]

One must have a sufficient aspiration and a prayer that is sufficiently intense. But that has been given to human nature. It is one of the marvellous gifts of grace given to human nature; only, one does not know how to make use of it.

This comes to saying that in spite of the most absolute determinisms in the horizontal line, if one knows how to cross all these horizontal lines and reach the highest point of consciousness, one is able to make things change, things apparently absolutely determined. So you may call it by any name you like, but it is a kind of combination of an absolute determinism with an absolute freedom. . . .

If you have an aspiration that is sincere enough or a prayer that is intense enough, you can bring down in you Something that will change everything, everything — truly it changes everything.[69]

Surrendering Responsibility

The Mother: Instead of being upset and struggling, the best thing to do is to offer one's body to the Divine with the *sincere* prayer, "Let Thy Will be done." If there is any possibility of cure, it will establish the best conditions for it; and if cure is impossible, it will be the very best preparation for getting out of the body and the life without it.

In any case the first indispensable condition is a quiet surrender to the Divine's will.[70]

Turn your mind completely away from your difficulty, concentrate exclusively on the Light and the Force coming from above; let the Lord do for your body whatever He pleases. Hand over to Him totally the entire responsibility of your physical being.

This is the cure.[71]

Be peaceful and quiet, give up the charge of everything to the Lord and you will be quite all right.[72]

I have been having trouble with my body for some time. . . .
A functioning is upset. . . . I don't know what it is.

(After a silence)

Because the Force of transformation is working very, very hard, and there are many people like that; the functions are no longer what you call "normal", that is, there is a change in the functioning, and so the first impression is always disorder. But if you can put into your body that kind of quiet patience, you know . . . which does not worry, after some time it is all right.... For example, for digestion, one day you cannot digest anything . . . and then if you stay *very quiet* like that, without worrying — especially without worrying — you see that it slowly takes on another movement, and then it is all right... but in another, quite new way. . . .

If you can manage to put into the body — *into* the body

— *complete* surrender, that is, that it *counts only* on the intervention of the Supreme, you understand; that the *body* — the
body — says to Him: "Here (*Mother opens her hands*), here..."
face to face with the Supreme, with the knowledge that He is
there; that He is there in the atmosphere, in the cells, in everything, and... (*gesture of open hands*) and that is all. That is
very effective.[73]

The Surrender of the Cells

The Mother: Suppose you have a pain somewhere; the instinct
(the instinct of the body, the instinct of the cells) is to shrink
and to seek to reject — that is the worst thing, that increases
it invariably. Therefore, the first thing to teach the body is to
remain immobile, to have no reaction; above all, no shrinking, not even a movement of rejection — a perfect immobility.
That is bodily equality.

A perfect immobility.

After the perfect immobility comes the movement of inner
aspiration (I am always speaking of the aspiration of the cells
— I use words for what no words can describe, but there is no
other way to express it), the surrender, that is to say, the *spontaneous and total* acceptance of the supreme Will.[74]

How to master physical suffering?

That is just the experience I am having now.

The body is in a state in which it sees that everything depends simply on how it is linked with the Divine — upon the
state of its receptive surrender. I have had the experience again
in the last few days. The same thing, which is the cause of a —
more than discomfort — a suffering, an almost unbearable
ailment, with just a change in the receptivity of the body towards the Divine, disappears all of a sudden — and can even

turn into a blissful state. I have had the experience many times. For me it is only a question of sincerity becoming intense — in the consciousness that everything is the action of the Divine and that his action moves towards the quickest possible realisation, given the conditions.

I might say: the cells of the body must learn to seek their support only in the Divine, until the moment when they are able to feel that they are the expression of the Divine. . . .

In a certain attitude (but it is difficult to explain or define), in a certain attitude all becomes divine. And there, what is wonderful is that when one has the experience of everything becoming divine, all that is contrary disappears quite naturally, quickly or slowly, instantaneously or little by little, depending on the thing.

That is indeed wonderful. That is to say, to become conscious that all is divine is the best way of making all divine — annulling all oppositions.[75]

Part Four

Medicine and Healing

Where the illness becomes pronounced and chronic in the body, it is necessary often to call in the aid of physical treatment and that is then used as a support of the Force.[1]

Sri Aurobindo

1

Medical Treatment
and the Body-Consciousness

The Mother: In most cases the use of medicines — within reasonable limits, that is, when one doesn't poison oneself by taking medicines — is simply to help the body to have confidence. It is the body which heals itself. When it wants to be cured, it is cured. And this is something very widely recognised now; even the most traditional doctors tell you, "Yes, our medicines help, but it is not the medicines which cure, it is the body which decides to be cured." Very well, so when the body is told, "Take this", it says to itself, "Now I am going to get better", and because it says "I am going to get better", well, it is cured!

In almost every case, there are things which help — a little — provided it is done within reasonable limits. If it is no longer within reasonable limits, you are sure to break down completely. You cure one thing but catch another which is usually worse. But still, a little help, in a way, a little something that gives confidence to your body — "Now it will be all right, now that I have taken this, it is going to be all right" — this helps it a great deal and it decides to get better and it is cured.

There too, there is a whole range of possibilities, from the yogi who is in so perfect a state of inner control that he could take poison without being poisoned to the one who at the least little scratch rushes to the doctor and needs all sorts of special drugs to get his body to make the movement needed for its cure. There is the whole possible range, from total, supreme mastery to an equally total bondage to all external aids and all that you absorb from outside — a bondage and a perfect liberation. There is the whole range. So everything is possible. It is like a great key-board, very complex and very complete, on which one can play, and the body is the instrument.[2]

Sri Aurobindo: As regards malady or illness, it is true that the chief reliance should be on the inner will and secondly on simple remedies. But this rule should not at first be rigorously applied in affections of a strongly physical character, because the gross body is the most obstinately recalcitrant to the will; there it is better in the earlier stages to respect to a certain extent the habits of the bodily consciousness which being physical relies upon physical remedies. When you find that the will is strong enough to deal rapidly with even these affections, then you can dispense with remedies.[3]

Physical Support for the Action of the Force

Sri Aurobindo: It is very good if one can get rid of illness entirely by faith and yoga-power or the influx of the Divine Force. But very often this is not altogether possible, because the whole nature is not open or able to respond to the Force. The mind may have faith and respond, but the lower vital and the body may not follow. Or, if the mind and vital are ready, the body may not respond, or may respond only partially, because it has the habit of replying to the forces which produce a particular illness, and habit is a very obstinate force in the material part of the nature. In such cases the use of the physical means can be resorted to, — not as the main means, but as a help or material support to the action of the Force. Not strong and violent remedies, but those that are beneficial without disturbing the body.[4]

Medicines are a *pis aller* [makeshift] that have to be used when something in the consciousness does not respond or responds superficially to the Force. Very often it is some part of the material consciousness that is unreceptive — at other times it is the subconscient which stands in the way even when the whole waking mind, life, physical consent to the liberating influence. If the subconscient also answers, then even a slight touch of the Force can not only cure the particular illness but make that form or kind of illness practically impossible hereafter.[5]

It is a fact of my experience that when the resistance in the body is too strong and persistent, it can help to take some aid of physical means as an instrumentation for the Force to work more directly on the body itself; for the body then feels itself supported against the resistance from both sides, by means both physical as well as supraphysical.[6]

The Mother: In every case, it is the Force that cures.

Medicines have little effect; it is the faith in medicines that cures.

Get treated by the doctor whom you trust and take only the medicines that inspire trust in you.

The body only has trust in material methods and that is why you have to give it medicines — but medicines have an effect only if the Force acts through them.[7]

It is quite evident that anything and everything can be cured by Grace and faith — but the faith in the Grace and its almighty power must be absolute and perfectly sincere and this condition is so rarely fulfilled that most often the necessity of a medical intervention is still there.[8]

What should be my attitude when prescribing medicines for my patients?

Give them medicines only when they *believe* in medicines themselves.[9]

One could say in conclusion that it is the faith of the patient which gives the remedy its power to heal.[10]

Alternative Healing Systems

Sri Aurobindo: I have seen the working of both the systems [Allopathy and Homeopathy] and of others and I can't believe in the sole truth of any. The ones damnable in the orthodox view, entirely contradicting it, have their own truth and succeed — also both the orthodox and heterodox fail. A theory is only a constructed idea-script which represents an imperfect human observation of a line of processes that Nature follows or can follow; another theory is a different idea-script of other processes that also she follows or can follow. Allopathy, homeopathy, naturopathy, osteopathy, Kaviraji [Ayurveda], Hakimi have all caught hold of Nature and subjected her to certain processes; each has its successes and failures. Let each do its work in its own way. I do not see any need for fights and recriminations. For me all are only outward means and what really works are unseen forces from behind; as they act, the outer means succeed or fail — if one can make the process a right channel for the right force, then the process gets its full vitality — that's all.[11]

Homeopathy is nearer to Yoga. Allopathy is more mechanical. Homeopathy deals with the physical personality — all the symptoms put together and making up this personality. Allopathy goes by diagnosis which does not consider the personality. The action of homeopathy is more subtle and dynamic.[12]

I am puzzled to think how such infinitesimal [homeopathic] doses in dilution can act on the human system.

That is no puzzle to me. Sometimes the infinitesimal is more powerful than the mass; it approaches more and more the subtle state and from the physical goes into a dynamic or vital state and acts vitally.[13]

To bring out the latent illness and counteract it is a recognised principle in homeopathy and is a principle in Nature itself.[14]

There are plenty of cases of illnesses being cured by other systems (not homeopathy alone) when they had defied the allopaths.[15]

The Mother: Allopaths ordinarily cure one thing, only to the detriment of another.

Ayurvedic doctors do not usually have this drawback. That is why I recommend them.[16]

Strong Drugs and Side-Effects

Sri Aurobindo: It is hardly possible to give a list of drugs [which should not be prescribed for sadhaks], but the general rule is that very strong or violent medicines should be avoided as much as possible — for Yoga increases the sensitivity of the vital and physical reactions and drugs tend to produce stronger or other effects than with ordinary persons.[17]

When a medicine is a specific, it is scientifically supposed to be active on one particular disease and therefore quite successful. . . . But you don't give your approval even though these medicines are specifics in these particular diseases.

It is not enough for a medicine to be a specific. Certain drugs have other effects or possible effects which can be ignored by the physician who only wants to cure his case, but cannot be in a whole-view of the system and its reactions.[18]

The Mother: I am against the indiscriminate use of *any* medicine, and when a medicine becomes fashionable there is a tendency to use it indiscriminately.[19]

An hour's moving about in the sun does more to cure weakness or even anaemia than a whole arsenal of tonics. My advice is that medicines should not be used unless it is absolutely impossible to avoid them; and this "absolutely impossible" should be very strict.[20]

The doctor gives me medicines — I observe the medicines: they cause as much disorder as they do good. They do good to one thing and harm to another. So afterwards that has to be set right. You never get out of it.[21]

Nature as Healer

The Mother: The more drugs you take, the more you undermine your body's natural resistance.[22]

Nature is the all-round Healer.[23]

Sri Aurobindo: Medicine is necessary for our bodies in disease only because our bodies have learned the art of not getting well without medicines. Even so, one sees often that the moment Nature chooses for recovery is that in which the life is abandoned as hopeless by the doctors.[24]

It is not the medicine that cures so much as the patient's faith in the doctor and the medicine. Both are a clumsy substitute for the natural faith in one's own self-power which they have themselves destroyed.[25]

For nearly forty years I believed them when they said I was weakly in constitution, suffered constantly from the smaller and the greater ailments and mistook this curse for a burden that Nature had laid upon me. When I renounced the aid of medicines, then they began to depart from me like disappointed parasites. Then only I understood what a mighty force was the natural health within me and how much mightier yet the Will and Faith exceeding mind which God meant to be the divine support of our life in this body.[26]

Medical Science and the Curative Power Within Us

Sri Aurobindo: The spirit within us is the only all-efficient doctor and submission of the body to it the one true panacea.[27]

Drugs often cure the body when they do not merely trouble or poison it, but only if their physical attack on the disease is supported by the force of the spirit; if that force can be made to work freely, drugs are at once superfluous.[28]

It should take long for self-cure to replace medicine, because of the fear, self-distrust and unnatural physical reliance on drugs which Medical Science has taught to our minds and bodies and made our second nature.[29]

The Mother: The sovereignty of mind has made humanity the slave of doctors and their remedies. And the result is that illnesses are increasing in number and seriousness.

The only true salvation for men is to escape from mental domination by opening to the Divine Influence.[30]

We cannot counteract the harm done by mental faith in the need for drugs by any external measures. Only by escaping from the mental prison and emerging consciously into the light of the spirit, by a conscious union with the Divine, can we enable Him to give back to us the balance and health we have lost.[31]

Diseases, Disorders and Doctors

The Mother: Doctors would not exist without diseases, you understand. I am not saying that they consciously encourage them, but they are on quite... friendly terms.

It is very subtle, but absolutely true.

I see a given vibratory phenomenon of the cells with the Consciousness (let us call it universal Consciousness), and then the very same thing seen in a medical consciousness — if you knew how changed it is! It takes on a very concrete character, to begin with (which it otherwise does not have), and then very... it is between "fatal" and "inescapable", I don't know how to explain. It is like a sort of rigid Fate. When they say, "Oh, it is an illness" — finished. And it is not true, there is no such thing as "an illness", no two cases are identical. . . .

I feel it clearly, you know: I have in me the possibility of five or six fatal diseases (I know it from the vibrations); if I had the misfortune, not to go to a hospital, but just to confide in a doctor, I would have incurable diseases. And this isn't against any doctor in particular (they themselves suffer from the atmosphere without knowing it): it is the medical atmosphere.

Disease is their *raison d'être*: without diseases there would be no doctors. There would be no need for them, they would be something else: they could become something else, but not doctors; something else very useful, I don't know — scientists of the human constitution, scientists of food utilisation, scientists of all sorts of things it is good to know, but not "doctors" — a doctor is for curing diseases, so there have to be diseases in order to have doctors.

And I am not quite sure that before doctors existed there were diseases — there were disorders, there were accidents, there were all sorts of things because all that exists, but there wasn't the *label* "disease". And the more learned doctors become (that is, the better they know their trade), the more (*Mother clenches her fist*) solid and fixed diseases become. So the doctors' usefulness is to cure them — without diseases, they wouldn't be useful.

They should be scientists of life.... The Chinese had that idea to some extent. I don't know how it is nowadays, but in the past each family had a doctor (a doctor could have a lot of families under his care), and the doctor was paid only when everyone was in good health — if someone was ill, they stopped paying him![32]

The minute you step into their hospitals, you are ill! That is right, it is as I say: it is the medical atmosphere. Jules Romains said it: "A healthy man is a man who does not know he is sick." So *a priori* you are sick — it goes without saying that you are sick. And if they don't immediately find what is wrong with you, it is because you have the knack of hiding it!

But, oh, how many little experiences I have had about this, and so interesting! Something is wrong here or there in the body, a small thing; as long as you don't pay attention to it — as long, above all, as you don't mention it to anyone — and you give it up to the Lord (if it happens to hurt, you give it up to the Lord), it is all right — it is fine, you aren't sick: it is "a disorder somewhere". If you are unfortunate enough to utter a word about it to anyone, and especially to the doctor, whoever he is, it instantly becomes an illness. And I know why, it is because the cells that are in disorder feel all of a sudden they are very important and very interesting persons! So then, as they are very interesting, they must make themselves still more interesting. If they have a movement that isn't harmonious, they exaggerate it — it becomes even less harmonious in order to assert itself more.

It sounds like a joke, but it is true! That is how it is, I know it. I have observed it carefully in my cells. So when they are told (*Mother slaps her armrest*), "You fools! That is not your duty at all, you are ridiculous," they keep quiet. As a drama, it is wonderful. . . .

The doctor crystallizes the illness, makes it concrete, hard. Afterwards, he takes credit for curing it... when he can![33]

Now that the body knows a little, when something is wrong or goes awry for some reason or other (it may be because of transformation, it may be because of attacks — there are innumerable reasons), my cells are beginning to say, "Oh, no doctor, no doctor, no doctor!..." They feel the doctor will crystallize the disorder, harden it and take away the plasticity necessary to respond to the deeper forces; and then the disorder will follow an outward, material course... which takes ages — I don't have the time to wait.

I never say this to people who ask me, never; I always tell them, "Go and see the doctor and do as he tells you." Because unless the body itself (some people have that, but not many, very few), if the body itself says, "No, no, no! I don't want," then it is ready; but if the body keeps telling you, "Maybe the doctor will help me out, maybe he will find..." — go ahead, go ahead! Do as he says.[34]

For a long time, would you believe it, I have been in search of a doctor, a man with full medical knowledge, knowing all that they now know about the human body and the way to cure it, *and* capable of having the contact with the higher consciousness. Because through such an instrument, one could do very, very interesting things — very interesting.

There is a domain in which "disease" and "cure" no longer exist, but only disorder, confusion, and harmony, organisation. . . . I would like, oh, I would very much like to discuss certain things or certain details of the body's functioning and organisation with a man who thoroughly knows anatomy, biology, physical and bodily chemistry — all those things thoroughly — and who *understands*, who is ready to understand that all those things are a projection of other forces, subtler forces; who is able to feel things as I feel them in my own body. That would be very interesting. . . .

You understand, to know all the material, cellular questions with the full knowledge of all the details, and at the same time to have that vision — if you could put both together, you would be... a divine doctor. That would be marvellous.[35]

2

Doctors and the Healing Power

Sri Aurobindo: A medical friend of the Mother's used to say that it is the doctor who heals and not his medicines. This is quite true. One must have an element of healing power. Medicines lend their properties to this power. Without this power which is the main thing in a cure, medicines are of very little use.[36]

You are very much behind the times. Do you not know that even many doctors now admit and write it publicly that medicines are an element but only one and that the psychological element counts as much and even more? I have heard that from doctors often and read it over reputable medical signatures. And among the psychological elements, they say, one of the most important is the doctor's optimism and self-confidence, (his faith, what? it is only another word for the same thing) and the confidence, hope, helpful mental atmosphere he can inspire in or around his patient. I have seen it stated categorically that a doctor who can do that is far more successful than one who knows Medicine better but cannot.[37]

Choosing One's Doctor

The Mother: To go from one doctor to another is the same mistake as to go from one Guru to another. One is on the material plane what the other is on the spiritual. You must choose your doctor and stick to him if you do not want to enter into physical confusion. It is only if the doctor himself decides to consult another or others that the thing can be done safely.[38]

Let him choose his doctor, because it is the *confidence* in the doctor that is *most important*.[39]

As a general rule I feel that when one goes to a doctor for treatment, one should do what he says.[40]

After all, an illness is only a wrong attitude taken by some part of the body. The chief role of the doctor is, by various means, to induce the body to recover its trust in the Supreme Grace.[41]

Qualities of a Doctor

Sri Aurobindo: Naturally one must know the business. But there is an enormous difference between a man who knows his business and has confidence and intuition and one who knows his business but has not. I have known doctors with an excellent knowledge of medicine who succeeded much less than others who had far less but had dash, decision and drive. . . .

The self-confident doctor decides as best he can and acts — if he finds he is making *fausse route* [on the wrong track], he retraces his steps and corrects. He develops in himself the *coup d'oeil* [ability to see at a glance] which does not depend only on reasoning and finally manages to be right in the majority of cases. You may say that he may kill his patients when he is wrong. But so does the hesitant doctor by his hesitation

— e.g. by not taking a step which is urgently required.[42]

The Mother: A broad mind, a generous heart, an unflinching will, a quiet steady determination, an inexhaustible energy and a total trust in one's mission — this makes a perfect doctor.[43]

To medical knowledge and experience, add full faith in the Divine's Grace and your healing capacity will have no limits.[44]

Yoga and the Practice of Medicine

Sri Aurobindo: If a sadhak can call down the force to cure him without need of medical treatment, that is always the best, but it is not always possible so long as the whole consciousness, mental, vital, physical down to the most subconscient is not open and awake. There is no harm in a doctor who is a sadhak carrying on his profession and using his medical knowledge; but he should do it in reliance on the Divine Grace and the Divine Will; if he can get true inspiration to aid his science, so much the better. No doctor can cure all cases. You are to do your best with the best result you can.[45]

As for medical treatment it is sometimes a necessity. If one can cure by the Force as you have often done it is the best — but if for some reason the body is not able to respond to the Force (e.g. owing to doubt, lassitude or discouragement or for inability to react against the disease), then the aid of medical treatment becomes necessary. It is not that the Force ceases to act and leaves all to the medicine, — it will continue to act through the consciousness but take the support of the treatment so as to act directly on the resistance in the body, which responds more readily to physical means in its ordinary consciousness.[46]

If we doctors are important as mediums, you must tell me what our attitude should be in conducting a case.

Faith, openness, an alert and flexible intelligence. I mean by faith especially faith as a dynamic means of bringing about what has to be effected or realised.

Can we help a patient by aspiring for him? Since the Divine Force is already acting on him, how can my aspiration help him further?

It can. Every little helps. . . .

I am still wondering why there should be doctors and a dispensary at all! Isn't it a paradox — the Divine sending his disciples to the human physician?

Rubbish! This is a world of the play of forces, sir, and the Doctor is a force. So why should not the Divine use him? Have you realised that if the Divine did everything, there would be no world, only a show of marionettes?[47]

It is faith that gets things done and even makes the impossible possible. But it has to be kept when even there is no immediate result. In the physical cure of a patient also there are adverse periods when the resistance is great and obstinate and there seems to be more swinging back than going forwards or a persistent recurrence of the trouble. Faith persisting and the call bring down after a time sufficient Force to overcome the obstacle.[48]

Do you think the Yogic Force will enable a doctor, even if he is not trained, to do things like cutting off an appendix or a cataract?

Good Heavens, no! Spare the poor people's eyes. The Force has to prepare its instrument first — it is not a miracle-monger. The Force can develop in you intuition and skill if you are sufficiently open, even if you did not have it before — but not like that. That kind of thing happens once in a way, but it is not the fixed method of the Divine to act like that.[49]

Why should I study all these diseases or go to the hospital? Can't I leave all that to Yogic force?

Yogic force is all right when one is in a Yogic condition, and when it acts. But when it does not, medicine is handy.[50]

You said in S's case that the Force has to count on right medicines for rapid effects.

I did not mean that it cannot be done without medicines. But if it is to be done with the aid of medicines, then the right medicine is helpful, the wrong one obviously brings in a danger.[51]

You yourself have said that if the diagnosis is correct and

appropriate medicines are administered the Force can work
quickly and effectively.

Yes, certainly. On the contrary, when there is a grave error in
the treatment, . . . then the Force has to fight that as well as
the illness, and it becomes difficult.[52]

The Doctor as an Instrument of the Divine

I am puzzled how a man with a big ego, like R, can be an
instrument of the Divine. . . . And yet R cures diseases won-
derfully. How is it that he is used as an instrument by the
Divine?

Sri Aurobindo: The Divine is there in all men, so the Divine
and the ego do live together. But the Divine is veiled by the
ego and manifests in proportion as the ego *first submits itself,*
then recedes and disappears. There can be no complete presence by the Divine without disappearance of the ego.

Any man can be an instrument of the Divine. . . . The thing
is to be a perfectly conscious instrument.[53]

He can cure the people all right, in spite of ego — the force
too does work through his vital and not his mind only, because his vital is strong, ardent and enthusiastic. Most people's vitals are half-dead things, busy only with their little
selfish desires. R's is at most vain and ambitious but not selfish — it is rather large and generous; therefore a good instrument.

Inner sadhana is another matter, there the ego stands as a
great obstacle.[54]

He is a man who seems genuinely to believe in the Force. . . .
So he has the first requisite of being a "medium" of Force.
Next, he is a man of great vital push, self-confidence, abound-
ing enthusiasm and energy; such men are the best instruments,
not for knowledge, but for successful action. Second requisite
there. Next, he is a man with a great power of suggestion and
also of inducing auto-suggestions in his patients, and these
become remarkably effective, provided they do not resist too
much. He is the kind of man who can give pure water, saying,
"This is a potent medicine", and the patient would immediately feel better after taking it. (By the way, many allopathic
doctors do that, when they think it necessary, according to
their own confession). Third help (though the trick would be
unYogic); the power of conveying one's own thought-formations, vital energy, will — decisions etc. to others being an
element in Yogic action: he has that. Fourth, a knowledge of
homeopathic medicines and what seems to me a very supple
and daring use of them. Dangerous? perhaps or rather, no
doubt; he himself admits that with his more potent medicines
a great disturbance occurs before the cure or can do so and a
great disturbance means a great risk; but a daring man is a
man who takes risks in the hope of great results. . . . An allopathic doctor also takes risks and those who are the most
successful are also the most adventurous and decisive in their
methods. All that does not militate against his capacity as a
healer. They are points in his favour.[55]

Immense energy, enthusiasm, vital force, 100 miles an hour
determination to succeed and a 2000 horse power confidence,
"I will do it" — vital absolutely convinced of the Force, mind
constantly finding reasons for belief in it . . . rapid intuitions
getting there in spite of any errors of speculation, decision of
mind and will accompanied by a mobile and plastic observing
mind suiting itself to the circumstances and then overcoming
them — that's the secret of a powerful instrumentalism — at

least in a rajasic man. A sattwic fellow would do it also but on other lines. . . .

The qualities you enumerate of the rajasic man's instrumentalism are more inborn than acquired it seems to me. . . . Even if acquired by Yoga, won't there be a difference between the instrumentalism of the one born with them and the other who has acquired them?

There may be a difference, but this is after all not a competitive examination. If one can be a good and strong instrument, that is enough.[56]

You have said, "A sattwic fellow would do it also but on other lines." Will you tell us how?

. . . The sattwic man would have less vital rush, more balance, harmony, even working out of the Force — he might do less surprising things or rather give them a less surprising appearance, but possibly he would be more quietly sure.[57]

The Force, the Instrument and the Instrumentation

Sri Aurobindo: The Force does not act in a void and in an absolute way, like writing on a blank paper or on the air the "Let there be Light and there was Light" formula. It comes as a Force intervening and acting on a very complex nexus of Forces that were in action and displacing their disposition and interrelated movement and natural result by a new disposition, movement and result.

It meets in so doing a certain opposition, very often a strong opposition from many of the forces already in possession and operation. To overcome it three factors are needed: (1) the power of the Force itself, i.e., its own sheer pressure and direct action on the field of action (here the man, his condition, his body); (2) the instrument (yourself [the doctor]); and (3) the instrumentation (treatment, medicine).

I have often used the Force alone, without any human instrument or outer means, but here all depends upon the recipient and his receptivity — unless, as in the case of healers, there are unseen beings or powers that assist.

If there is an instrument in direct touch with the patient, whether the doctors or one who can canalise the Force, then the action is immensely assisted, — how much depends on the instrument, his faith, his energy, his conveying power. Where there is a violent opposition, this is frequently not enough, or at least not enough for a rapid or total effect, the instrumentation (treatment or medicine) is needed. It is especially where the resistance of the body or the forces acting on the body-consciousness is strong that the medicine comes in as an aid.

But if the doctor is non-psychic or the medicine the wrong one or the treatment unplastic, then they become added resistance which the Force has to overcome.

This is a summary and a very inadequate statement, but it gives the main points, I believe.

P.S. I forgot to say that the surroundings, especially the people around the patient, the atmosphere, the suggestions it carries or they give to him, are often of a considerable importance.[58]

My role in a medical case is to use the force either with or without medicines. There are three ways of doing that — one by putting the Force without knowing or caring what the illness is or following the symptoms — that however needs either the mental collaboration or acquiescence of the victim. The second is symptomatic, to follow the symptoms and act on them even if one is not sure of the disease. There an accurate report is very useful. The third needs a diagnosis — that is usually where the anti-forces are very strong and conscious or where the patient himself answers strongly to the suggestions of the illness and unwittingly resents the action of the Force. This last is usually indicated by the fact that the thing gets cured and comes back again or improves and swings back again to worse. It is especially the great difficulty in cases of insanity and the like. Also in things where the nerves have a say — but in ordinary illnesses too.[59]

As to Force let me point out a few elementary notions. . . .

    1. The Force is a divine Force, so obviously it can apply itself in any direction; it can inspire the poet, set in motion the soldier, doctor, scientist, everybody.

    2. The Force is not a mental Force — it is not bound to go out from the Communicator with every detail mentally arranged, precise in its place, and communicate it mentally to the Recipient. It can go out as a global Force containing in itself the thing to be done, but working out the details in the Recipient and the action as the action progresses. It is not necessary for the Communicant to accompany mentally the Force, plant himself mentally in the mind of the Recipient and work out mentally there the details. He can send the Force or put on the Force, leave it to do its work and attend himself to other matters. In the world most things are worked out by such a global Force containing the results in itself, but involved, concealed, and working them out in a subsequent operation. The seed contains the whole potentiality of the tree, the gene contains the potentiality of the living form that it initiates, etc., etc., but if you examine the seed and gene *ad infinitum*, still you will not find there either the tree or the living being. All the same the Force has put all these potentialities there in a certain evolution which works itself out automatically.

    3. In the case of a man acting as an instrument of the Force the action is more complicated, because consciously or unconsciously the man must receive, also he must be able to work out what the Force puts through him. He is a living complex

instrument, not a simple machine. So if he has responsiveness, capacity etc. he can work out the Force perfectly, if not he does it imperfectly or frustrates it. That is why we speak of and insist on the perfectioning of the instrument. Otherwise there would be no need of Sadhana or anything else — any fellow would do for any blessed work and one would simply have to ram things into him and see them coming out into action.

4. The Communicant need not be an all-round many-sided Encyclopaedia in order to communicate the Force for various purposes. . . . Naturally the best instrument even is imperfect (unless he is a perfected Adhar), and mistakes may be committed, other suggestions accepted etc., etc., but if the instrument is sufficiently open, the Force can set the thing to rights and the result still comes. In some or many cases the Force has to be renewed from time to time or supported by fresh Force. In some directions particular details have to be consciously attended to by the Communicant. All that depends on circumstances too multitudinous and variable to be reduced to rule. There are general lines, in these matters, but no rules; the working of a non-mental Force has necessarily to be plastic, not rigid and tied to formulas. If you want to reduce things to patterns and formulas, you will necessarily fail to understand the workings of a spiritual (non-mental) Force.[60]

The Collaboration of the Patient

Sri Aurobindo: As for saving, one can't save if the patient cherishes the illness, justifies it and refuses to part with it. . . .

What does save is the true will to be saved accompanied by a reliance on the Divine.[61]

If you can get the preoccupation of death and grave illness out of his head, that might help. It is his sense of being desperately ill that prevents the force working.[62]

Do you think that X could have been cured? Most people believe that cancer is incurable.

It was possible in his case, at least; but something in him ceased to respond. . . . The last three days his body did not respond either to the force put upon him, or to the medicine given.

Could not the spiritual help be effective irrespective of his response?

In cases like this the entire collaboration of the person concerned is absolutely necessary.

But if you know the force that is attacking?

To detect the force that is attacking is one thing and to drive it out is another. In these cases the mind plays a very great part. . . .

What are the conditions for success in such cases?

Either entire collaboration or complete passivity. These are the two conditions for a cure.[63]

Curing "Incurable" Illnesses

The Mother: The cells of the body get the habit of increasing without cause. This is cancer. If you change the consciousness in the cells and get rid of their habit, cancer can be cured.[64]

Sri Aurobindo: [Regarding a woman with cancer:] It is evident that it is a dangerous illness, not easily curable — but we cannot say positively either that she will not survive. There is no such thing as an incurable illness in reality — for what the doctors call such is only an illness for which they have not yet been able to discover a physical remedy. X has one force on her side, her faith and her will to survive for the sadhana; on the other side is a kind of destiny of the body which is strong but not absolutely unsurmountable. Her faith must be left intact — and we must send force to help her, that is all that we can say at present. If she can by her faith draw down and open to such a force as will counteract the adverse physical forces on her body, then she will survive.[65]

Of course it can [cancer can be cured by yoga], but on condition of faith or openness or both. Even a mental suggestion can cure cancer — with luck of course, as is shown by the case of the woman operated on unsuccessfully for cancer, but the doctors lied and told her it had succeeded. Result, cancer symptoms all ceased and she died many years afterwards of another illness altogether.[66]

A successful cure of X's mother would be certainly a considerable achievement and though difficult owing to the tenacity and malignance and extreme intractability of the disease, it is not impossible. What you say is true, the Force was acting before, but it acted with immediate rapidity and completeness only with those who had sufficient faith and receptivity (mainly Sadhaks) or in other good conditions.

These cases seem to indicate a new power of the Force and a new technique. Your idea that it may spread and happen elsewhere is not without foundation; for, when once something is there in the earth-atmosphere that was not there before, it begins to work on many sides in an unforeseen way. Thus, since the Yoga has been in action, its particular opening movements have come to a number of people who were at a distance and not connected with us and who understood nothing of what was happening to them. These things are to be expected for Nature is still in evolution and new Lights and Powers have to be brought down in her and made part of the conscious earth-existence.[67]

3

Intuitive Diagnosis

The Mother: You can see ten people [doctors], those ten people will tell you ten different things! The instability of the diagnosis is for me something absolutely certain. Because there aren't two identical cases — there are analogies, there can even be families of cases, but there aren't two identical cases; so in everyone there are variations. And unless the gentleman is very intuitive, he will start reasoning and then he is sure to make a mistake. . . .

I have known one or two sincere doctors, and they admitted to me quite clearly that it was like that. I told them, "From the spiritual standpoint, there cannot be two identical cases. Nature never repeats itself — there are families, there are analogies, there are similarities, but there aren't two identical cases; therefore you know very well that you don't know. When you study it on its own level, the immense complexity of the possibilities of physical reality is such that unless you have a direct and intimate perception, you cannot know what will happen."[68]

No two illnesses are alike, though labels are put on diseases and attempts made to group them; but in fact every person is ill in his own way, and his way depends on what he is, on his state of consciousness and the life he leads.[69]

Sri Aurobindo: What the Mother says in the matter is what she said to Dr. X with his entire agreement — viz. reading from symptoms by the doctors is usually mere balancing between possibilities (of course except in clear and simple cases) and the conclusion is a guess. It may be a right guess and then it will be all right or it may be a wrong guess and then all will be wrong unless Nature is too strong for the doctor and overcomes the consequences of his error — or at the least the treatment will be ineffective. On the contrary if one develops the diagnostic flair one can see at once what is the real thing among the possibilities and see what is to be done. That is what the most successful doctors have, they have this flashlight which shows them the true point. X agreed and said that the cause of the guessing was that there were whole sets of symptoms which could belong to any one of several diseases and to decide is a most delicate and subtle business, no amount of book knowledge or reasoning will ensure a right decision. A special insight is needed that looks through the symptoms and not merely at them. This last sentence, by the way, is my own, not X's.[70]

I was under the impression that it is quite possible to know intuitively, with the Yogic vision, the exact condition of a patient without any medical diagnosis, but from your recent remarks about some patients I find that it is not so. On the contrary you say that the Force can act better and quicker when there is a proper diagnosis. In that case you depend upon human instruments which being fallacious and ignorant mostly, will paralyse or baffle the working of the Force.

It can [the Yogic vision can know the condition of the patient intuitively] if you can train it to act in that field and if you can make it the real Intuition which sees the things without ranging among potentialities.

As for me, I have no medico in me, not even a latent medico. If I had, I would not need an external one but diagnose, prescribe and cure all by my solitary self. . . .

But if Yogic vision and knowledge can at once see a man through and through, his past, present and future, why can it not see this?

To see what is in a man is quite a different matter — it is the direct sphere of Yogic vision. As for all past, present, future, one does not see that at a glance, one comes to know little by little if one has a special faculty and cares to use it. These things are not miraculous, they are forces and faculties like others.[71]

I myself cure more often by attacking the symptoms than by any other way, because medical diagnosis is uncertain and fallible while the symptoms are there for everybody to see. Of course if a correct indisputable diagnosis is there, so much the better — the view can be more complete, the action easier, the result more sure. But even without infallible diagnosis one can act and get a cure.[72]

A symptomatic treatment can't be applied in cases where the same symptom is produced by two or three different diseases because the symptoms will always recur so long as one doesn't go to the root.

Why can't it? There is a possibility that you can strike at the cure, whatever it be, through the symptoms and you can kill the root through the stalk and leaves and not start by searching for the roots and digging them out. That at any rate is what I do.[73]

Mental Intuition and Yogic Intuition

You told me that Dr. R uses mental intuition. So there must be various levels of intuition.

Sri Aurobindo: By mental intuition I mean that the intuition coming from above gets mixed with the mind. I don't say that mental intuition must be incorrect but because of the mixture it can't always be relied upon. There is also vital intuition, which very often gets mixed up with one's desires.

How is one to get intuition? By calmness of mind?

Calmness is not enough. The mind must become silent. . . . One can train one's mind to be silent.[74]

Mental intuitive knowledge catches directly some aspect of the truth but without any completeness or certitude and the intuition is easily mixed with ordinary mental stuff that may be erroneous; in application it may easily be a half-truth or be so misinterpreted and misapplied as to become an error. Also, the mind easily imitates the intuition in such a way that it is difficult to distinguish between a true or a false intuition. That is the reason why men of intellect distrust the mental intuition and say that it cannot be accepted or followed unless it is tested and confirmed by the intellect.[75]

For ancient things like Ayurveda I don't believe in this modern system of schools and colleges. They make the whole thing mental and intellectual, while the ancient systems were more intuitive. In India they used to hand down such things from Guru to disciple. It is the same with Yoga. One can't think of Yogic schools and classes.[76]

Some people have a faculty for receiving impressions about others which is not by any means infallible, but often turns out to be right. That is one thing and the yogic intuition . . . is another. The first may help for developing the other, but it is not the same thing.[77]

It is possible to cultivate and extend the use of the intuitive mind in proportion as we rely less predominantly upon the reasoning intelligence. We may train our mentality not to seize, as it does now, upon every separate flash of intuitive illumination for its own inferior purposes, not to precipitate our thought at once into a crystallising intellectual action around it; we can train it to think in a stream of successive and connected intuitions, to pour light upon light in a brilliant and triumphant series. We shall succeed in this difficult change in proportion as we purify the interfering intelligence, — if we can reduce in it the element of material thought enslaved to the external appearances of things, the element of vital thought enslaved to the wishes, desires, impulses of the lower nature, the element of intellectual thought enslaved to our preferred, already settled or congenial ideas, conceptions, opinions, fixed operations of intelligence, if, having reduced to a minimum those elements, we can replace them by an intuitive vision and sense of things, an intuitive insight into appearances, an intuitive will and intuitive ideation.[78]

The Mother: If you want to contact the intuition, you must keep this (*Mother indicates the forehead*) completely immobile. Active thought must be stopped as far as possible and the entire mental faculty must form — at the top of the head and a little further above if possible — a kind of mirror, very quiet, very still, turned upwards, in silent, very concentrated attention. If you succeed, you can — perhaps not immediately — but you can have the perception of the drops of light fall-

ing upon the mirror from a still unknown region and expressing themselves as a conscious thought which has no connection with all the rest of your thought since you have been able
to keep it silent. That is the real beginning of the intellectual
intuition.

It is a discipline to be followed. For a long time one may
try and not succeed, but as soon as one succeeds in making a
"mirror", still and attentive, one always obtains a result, not
necessarily with a precise form of thought but always with
the sensations of a light coming from above. And then, if one
can receive this light coming from above without entering
immediately into a whirl of activity, receive it in calm and silence and let it penetrate deep into the being, then after a while
it expresses itself either as a luminous thought or as a very
precise indication here (*Mother indicates the heart*), in this
other centre. . . .

There comes a time when one feels a kind of inner guidance, something which is leading one very perceptibly in all
that one does. But then, for the guidance to have its maximum power, one must naturally add to it a conscious surrender: one must be sincerely determined to follow the indication
given by the higher force.[79]

Prognostications

Sri Aurobindo: Why do people make such prognostications?
Suggestions of the kind ought never to be made, mentally even
— they might act like suggestions and do more harm than any
good medicines could do. . . .

> *I am surprised to hear that even "prognostications" are
> very harmful. I thought these beliefs were just supersti-
> tions.*

Prognostications of that kind should not be lightly thought or
spoken . . . even if there is a possibility or probability, they

should be kept confidential from the person affected, unless it is necessary to inform. This is because of the large part played by state of consciousness and suggestion in illness.[80]

When we have spoken the truth, should we withdraw it if the other person gets depressed or troubled by it?

No. If it is true, it should not be withdrawn. But the truth need be told only when it helps the person spoken to, otherwise silence is better.[81]

The Mother: Do not let the doctor's words disturb you. Illnesses are never serious unless we accept them as such. Besides, I expect to hear very soon that you are better.[82]

[Should a doctor tell a patient the truth about a terminal illness?]

Obviously, there could be only one solution: to lose the mental consciousness that gives you the perception or sensation that you are telling a "lie" or a "truth"; and you can obtain that only when you get to the higher state in which our notion of falsehood and truth disappears. Because when we speak from the ordinary mental consciousness, even when we are convinced that we are telling the whole truth, we are not doing so; and even when we think we are telling a lie, sometimes it isn't one. We do not have the capacity to discern what is true and what isn't — because we live in a false consciousness.

But there is a state in which, first, you no longer make "personal" decisions, and then you are like a mirror reflecting the exact *need*, the true (spiritual, that is) need of the patient, for instance, and exactly when he needs to know so that the rest of his life (whatever time he has left to live) brings him the maximum possibilities of progress. . . .

In my opinion, from a practical and external standpoint, I have more often seen cases in which the lie had a bad effect than cases in which the truth had a bad effect. But everything depends on the doctor's consciousness.

I know, and with certainty, that if you can be in that clear consciousness, you will see that the state of illness was certainly a necessity, often a *willed* necessity (not only accepted and undergone, but willed) by the soul in order to go faster on the path — to save time, to gain lives. And if you can, if you have the power to bring that soul into contact with the force that governs its existence and leads it towards progress, towards the Realisation, you do a work of quite a superior quality.

You know this: the *same* words, the *same* sentences, spoken by someone who sees and knows and spoken by the ordinary ignorant person, change entirely in nature and power — and in action. There is a way of saying things which is the true way, whatever words you speak. . . .

You see, he puts the problem from a purely mental standpoint: to tell what is conventionally called the "truth" (which isn't true), or to tell what is conventionally called a "lie" (which may not at all be what you think it is: it isn't a lie, but simply the contradiction or opposite of what you consider to be the "truth" — same thing). But in order to find the solution, you have to climb up there — where you *see*, where you can see in a totally concrete way that that "truth" isn't absolute and that "lie" isn't absolute, that there is something else — another way of seeing — in which things are no longer like that.

And then... then if you could speak the True Thing, the right word (word or sentence), have the thought which is the *true* thought in every case — what marvellous power you would have over your patient! It would be magnificent.[83]

4

Spiritual Healing

Mother, is it possible to develop in oneself the capacity to heal?

The Mother: In principle, everything is possible by uniting consciously with the Divine Force.

But a method has to be found, and this depends on the case and the individual.

The first condition is to have a physical nature that gives energy rather than draws energy from others.

The second indispensable condition is to know how to draw energy from above, from the inexhaustible impersonal source.

In this way the more one spends the more one receives, and one becomes an inexhaustible channel rather than a vessel that empties itself by giving.

It is through steadfast aspiration that one learns.[84]

Healing comes not from the head but from the heart.[85]

Use of Spiritual Force

Sri Aurobindo: Spiritual force has its own concreteness; it can take a form (like a stream, for instance) of which one is aware and can send it quite concretely on whatever object one chooses.

This is a statement of fact about the power inherent in spiritual consciousness. But there is also such a thing as a willed use of any subtle force — it may be spiritual, mental or vital — to secure a particular result at some point in the world. Just as there are waves of unseen physical forces (cosmic waves etc.) or currents of electricity, so there are mind-waves, thought-currents, waves of emotion, — for example, anger, sorrow, etc., — which go out and affect others without their knowing whence they come or that they come at all, they only feel the result. One who has the occult or inner senses awake can feel them coming and invading him. Influences good or bad can propagate themselves in that way; that can happen without intention and naturally, but also a deliberate use can be made of them. There can also be a purposeful generation of force, spiritual or other. There can be too the use of the effective will or idea acting directly without the aid of any outward action, speech or other instrumentation which is not concrete in that sense, but is all the same effective. These things are not imaginations or delusions or humbug, but true phenomena.[86]

As for those who can live in the true Divine Consciousness, certain powers are not powers at all in that sense, not, that is to say, supernatural or abnormal, but rather their normal way of seeing and acting, part of the consciousness. . . .

Abnormal, otherwise supraphysical experiences and powers, occult or yogic, have always seemed to me something perfectly natural and credible. Consciousness in its very nature could not be limited by the ordinary physical human-animal consciousness, it must have other ranges.[87]

The Divine Forces are meant to be used — the mistake of man individualised in the Ignorance is to use it for the ego and not for the Divine. It is that that has to be set right by the union with the Divine Consciousness and also by the widening of the individual being so that it can live consciously in the universal. Difficult it is owing to the fixed ego-habit, but it is not impossible.[88]

Methods and Conditions of Effective Healing

The Mother: There are two ways of curing an illness spiritually. One consists in putting a force of consciousness and truth on the physical spot which is affected. In this case the effect produced depends naturally on the receptivity of the person. Supposing the person is receptive; the force of consciousness is put upon the affected part and its pressure restores order. Many of you here can tell how Sri Aurobindo cured them. It was like a hand which came and took away the pain. It is as clear as that.

In other cases, if the body lacks receptivity altogether or if its receptivity is insufficient, one sees the inner correspondence with the psychological state which has brought about the illness and acts on that. But if the cause of the illness is refractory, not much can be done. Let us say the origin is vital. The vital absolutely refuses to change, it clings enormously to the condition in which it is; then that is hopeless. You put the force, and usually it provokes an increase in the illness, produced by the resistance of the vital which did not want to accept anything. I speak of the vital but it can be the mind or something else.

When the action is directly upon the body, that is, on the affected part, it is possible that one is relieved; then, some hours later or even after a few days, the illness returns. This means that the cause has not been changed, that the cause is in the vital and is still there; it is only the effect which has been cured. But if one can act simultaneously upon both the cause and the effect, and the cause is sufficiently receptive to consent to change, then one is completely cured, once and for all.[89]

It is a question of receptivity. I am doing the best that can be done for him, but he goes on thinking that he is ill. All the time he is busy with that idea and he has made a strong formation of illness around him. He is unable to receive my help because of this formation. Let him discard the idea of illness and more than half the trouble will be over and it will be easy to cure him.[90]

I know too well the true reason of all these complications and this suffering to give him any advice, because it is only an inner and radical change of his character that can put an end to the ordeal. He has had with him and still has a conscious and steady concentration of force which ought to have cured him long ago. But his inner pessimism and dissatisfaction constantly spoil the working.

Let him have a true faith and then everything will be all right.[91]

One can cure only if the disease isn't necessary to the individual's development.[92]

Healing with the Hands

It is said that Christ used to heal simply by a touch. Is such healing possible?

Sri Aurobindo: Why not? There are many instances of such cures. No doubt, faith is necessary. Christ himself said, "Thy faith has made thee whole."[93]

The Mother: A told me that when he had a pain, he just had to put his hand on it and concentrate — it goes away. . . .

But concentrate in what way? You put your hand on, and then what? You call. . .

You put your hand on and you concentrate on... what you conceive as a higher force — either a Force of Harmony or a Force of Order. You put it on and you feel, it goes by like that and then it enters.

I believe every human being has that possibility. In any case, it always seemed a very natural thing to me. And when you develop it, it develops like anything else. Naturally when it takes on miraculous proportions, it is different.

But it is very instinctive. I don't know, even when I was very small, if I had a pain somewhere or a toothache, I used to do it — and when you are very small, you don't think anything about it — I did it like this (*Mother presses her cheek*), and then that brings relief.[94]

[Regarding a flower with the significance "Material Power to Heal"]

I would like that to be permanently established. When someone tells me, "I have a pain here", I pass my hand like this and it is gone.

The hands feel, they feel it is possible. They are so conscious of the Vibration — they feel that anything is possible. The other day, E fell down, I don't know how, and she injured her knee, she was covered with bruises and scratches. . . . Then this hand [Mother's right hand] quite spontaneously went and passed over her knee, like that, and I felt all the vibrations at my fingertips: it is like needles — needles of light — and it vibrates and vibrates and vibrates. So I put my hand like that, and suddenly she said, "Oh!..." She was flabbergasted: all the pain had gone.

But there were marks, bruises — they should go, but it takes time. On me the effect is almost immediate, especially the right hand.

But I would like it to have a sort of absoluteness. Because the decision to intervene isn't mental at all: suddenly the hand is simply compelled to do it, so it does it. Well, in that case, it should be absolute.... There is still the influence of the others' thought and all that, what a useless jumble![95]

I have seen Sri Aurobindo . . . when someone came to him with an acute pain somewhere: "Oh, it hurts here! Oh, it hurts! Oh!..." He said nothing, he remained calm, he looked at the person, and I saw, I saw something like a subtle physical hand which came and took hold of the little point dancing about in disorder and confusion, and he took it like this (*gesture*) and there, everything had gone.

"Oh, oh! Look my pain has gone."[96]

Thought-Formations and Praying for Others

Sri Aurobindo: To want unwaveringly the welfare of another both in the head and the heart, is the best help one can give.[97]

Yes, one's bad thoughts and good thoughts can have a bad or a good effect on others, though they have not always because they are not strong enough — but still that is the tendency. It is therefore always said by those who have this knowledge that we should abstain from bad thoughts of others for this reason. It is true that both kinds of thought come equally to the mind in its ordinary state; but if the mind and mental will are well developed, one can establish a control over one's thoughts as well as over one's acts and prevent the bad ones from having their play. But this mental control is not enough for the sadhak. He must attain to a quiet mind and in the silence of the mind receive only the Divine thought-forces or other divine Forces and be their field and instrument.[98]

Thoughts have an effective power — usually by creating an atmosphere or tendencies — thus when one is ill, those around should not have thoughts of gloomy foreboding, grief or fear, for that works against cure. But the capacity of conscious thought-formation is a special power and uncommon. It can be acquired or come of itself by sadhana.[99]

The Mother: Note that this power of formation has a great advantage, if one knows how to use it. You can make good formations and if you make them properly, they will act in the same way as the others. You can do a lot of good to people just by sitting quietly in your room, perhaps even more good than by undergoing a lot of trouble externally. If you know how to think correctly, with force and intelligence and kindness, if you love someone and wish him well very sincerely, deeply, with all your heart, that does him much good, much more certainly than you think. I have said this often; for example, to those who are here, who learn that someone in their family is very ill and feel that childish impulse of wanting to rush immediately to the spot to attend to the sick person. I tell you, unless it is an exceptional case and there is nobody to attend on the sick person (and at times even in such a case), if you know how to keep the right attitude and concentrate with affection and good will upon the sick person, if you know how to pray for him and make helpful formations, you will do him much more good than if you go to nurse him, feed him, help him wash himself — in short, all the things anybody can do. Anybody can nurse a person. But not everybody can make good formations and send out forces that act for healing.[100]

Without conscious occult powers, is it possible to help or
protect from a distance somebody in difficulty or danger?
If so, what is the practical procedure?
    What can thought do?

We are not going to speak of occult processes at all; although,
to tell the truth, everything that happens in the invisible world
is occult, by definition. But still, practically, there are two processes which do not exclude but complete each other, but which
may be used separately according to one's preference.

It is obvious that thought forms a part of one of the methods, quite an important part. I have already told you several
times that if one thinks clearly and powerfully, one makes a
mental formation, and that every mental formation is an entity independent of its fashioner, having its own life and tend-
ing to realise itself in the mental world — I don't mean that
you see your formation with your physical eyes, but it exists
in the mental world, it has its own particular independent existence. If you have made a formation with a definite aim, its
whole life will tend to the realisation of this aim. Therefore,
if you want to help someone at a distance, you have only to
formulate very clearly, very precisely and strongly the kind of
help you want to give and the result you wish to obtain. That
will have its effect. I cannot say that it will be all-powerful,
for the mental world is full of innumerable formations of this
kind and naturally they clash and contradict one another;
hence the strongest and the most persistent will have the best
of it.

Now, what is it that gives strength and persistence to mental
formations? It is emotion and will. If you know how to add to
your mental formation an emotion, affection, tenderness, love,
and an intensity of will, a dynamism, it will have a much greater
chance of success. That is the first method. It is within the

scope of all those who know how to think, and even more of those who know how to love. But as I said, the power is limited and there is great competition in that world.

Therefore, even if one has no knowledge at all but has trust in the divine Grace, if one has the faith that there is something in the world like the divine Grace, and that this something can answer a prayer, an aspiration, an invocation, and then, after making one's mental formation, if one offers it to the Grace and puts one's trust in it, asks it to intervene and has the faith that it will intervene, then indeed one has a chance of success.

Try, and you will surely see the result.

But Mother, when one prays sincerely for the intervention of the Grace, doesn't one expect a particular result?

Excuse me, that depends on the tenor of the prayer. If one simply invokes the Grace, or the Divine, and puts oneself in His hands, one does not expect a particular result. To expect a particular result one must formulate one's prayer, must ask for something. If you have only a great aspiration for the divine Grace and evoke it, implore it, without asking it for anything precise, it is the Grace which will choose what it will do for you, not you.

That is better, isn't it?

Ah! that is quite another question.

Why, it is higher in its quality, perhaps. But still, if one wants something precise, it is better to formulate it. If one has a special reason for invoking the Grace, it is better to formulate it precisely and clearly.

Of course, if one is in a state of complete surrender and gives oneself entirely, if one simply offers oneself to the Grace and lets it do what it likes, that is very good. But after that one must not question what it does! One must not say to it, "Oh! I did that with the idea of having this", for if one really has the idea of obtaining something, it is better to formulate it in all sincerity, simply, just as one sees it. Afterwards, it is for the Grace to choose if it will do it or not; but in any case, one will have formulated clearly what one wanted. And there is no harm in that.[101]

Conclusion

Beyond Illness and Healing

All shall be captured by delight, transformed:
In waves of undreamed ecstasy shall roll
Our mind and life and sense and laugh in a light
Other than this hard limited human day,
The body's tissues thrill apotheosised,
Its cells sustain bright metamorphosis.[1]

Sri Aurobindo

1

The Transformation of Suffering

Why is there suffering?

The Mother: . . . Because that is the only kind of vibration that can pull Matter out of its inertia.

The supreme Peace and Calm have been deformed and disfigured into inertia and *tamas*, and precisely because this was the deformation of true Peace and Calm, there was no reason why it should change. A certain vibration of awakening — of reawakening — was necessary in order to come out of this *tamas*; it could not pass directly into Peace. Something was needed to shake the *tamas*, and that was translated outwardly by suffering.

I am speaking here of physical suffering, because all the other forms of suffering — vital, mental, emotional suffering — are due to a wrong working of the mind, and these may simply be classified as Falsehood, nothing more. But physical suffering gives me the impression of a child being beaten, because here, in Matter, Falsehood has become ignorance; that is to say, there is no bad will — there is no bad will in Matter, all is inertia and ignorance. . . . This ignorance is everywhere in the cells, and it is only the experience — and the experience of what is translated in this rudimentary consciousness as suffering — that can awaken, arouse the need to know and to cure, and the aspiration to transform oneself.

. . . When something is disturbed in the functioning — that is to say, instead of being supple, spontaneous, natural, it becomes a painful effort . . . at that moment, the intensity of the aspiration, the call, increases tenfold, becomes constant. The difficulty is to remain in that state of intensity. Generally everything falls back, I would not say into a somnolence, but into a sort of relaxation: you take things easy, and it is only when the inner disorder becomes painful that the intensity grows and becomes permanent. For hours — hours together — without slackening, the call, the aspiration, the will to be united with the Divine, to become the Divine, is maintained at its maximum. Why? Because there was outwardly what is called a physical disorder, a suffering. Otherwise, when there is no suffering, from time to time one soars up, then one falls back into a relaxation of the intensity; then another time one soars up once more.... There is no end to it! It could continue forever. If we want things to go fast (relatively fast according to the rhythm of our life), this crack of the whip is necessary. I am convinced of it, because as soon as you are within your inner being you look upon that with contempt (as regards oneself).

But then, all of a sudden, when there comes this true Compassion of the Divine Love, and when one sees all these things that appear so horrible, so abnormal, so absurd, this great pain which is upon all beings and even upon all things... then there takes birth in this physical being the aspiration to soothe, to cure, to remove that. There is in Love, at its Origin, something which is translated constantly as the intervention of Grace: a force, a sweetness, something like a vibration of solace spread everywhere, but which an illumined consciousness can direct, concentrate on some points. And it is there, there itself that I saw the true use one can make of thought: thought serves as a kind of channel to carry this vibration from place to place, wherever it is necessary. This force, this vibration of sweetness is there in a static way upon the world, pressing in order to be received, but it is an impersonal action. And thought — illumined thought, surrendered thought, thought which is no longer anything but an instrument, which tries no longer to initiate things, which is satisfied with being moved by the higher Consciousness — thought serves as an intermediary to establish a contact, a relation, and to enable this impersonal Force to act wherever it is necessary, upon definite points.

It may be said without qualification that an affliction always carries with it its own remedy. You might say that the cure of each suffering coexists with the suffering. So instead of seeing a "useless", "stupid" affliction as one usually does, you see that the progress, the evolution which has made the suffering necessary — which is its cause and the reason for its existence — achieves the intended result; and at the same time the suffering is cured, for those who can open themselves and receive. The three things — suffering as a means of progress, progress, and the cure of suffering — are coexistent, simultaneous; that is to say, they do not follow each other, they take place at the same time.

If, at the moment when the transformative action creates a suffering, there is in that which suffers the necessary aspiration and opening, the remedy is received at the same time and the result is total, complete: transformation, with the working necessary to bring it about, and, at the same time, cure of the false sensation produced by the resistance. And the suffering is replaced by... something that is not known upon this earth, but is akin to joy, well-being, trust and security. It is a super-sensation, in a perfect peace, and clearly the only thing that can last eternally.

This analysis expresses very imperfectly what one would call the "content" of Ananda.

I believe it is something that has been felt and experienced, partially and very fleetingly, throughout the ages, but that it is just beginning to concentrate and almost concretise itself upon earth.[2]

Suffering as an Opportunity for Growth

The Mother: We were saying the other day that it is only his friends whom God treats severely. You thought it was a joke, but it is true. It is only to those who are full of hope, who can pass through this purifying flame, that the conditions for attaining the maximum result are given. And the human mind is made in such a way that you can test this. When something extremely unpleasant happens to you, you can tell yourself, "Well, this proves I am worth the trouble of being given this difficulty, this proves there is something in me that can withstand the difficulty", and you will notice that instead of tormenting yourself, you rejoice — you will be so happy and so strong that even the most unpleasant things will seem quite charming to you! This is a very easy experiment to make. Whatever the circumstance, if your mind gets in the habit of regarding it as something favourable, it will no longer be unpleasant for you. This is very well known: so long as the mind refuses to accept something, fights against it, tries to prevent it, there are torments, difficulties, storms, inner struggles and all kinds of suffering. But the minute the mind says, "Good, this is what has to happen, this is how it is to be", whatever happens, you are content. There are people who have acquired such control of their mind over their body that they feel nothing.[3]

If you can face suffering with courage, endurance, an unshakable faith in the divine Grace, if instead of shunning it when it comes to you, you can enter into it with this will, this aspiration to go through it and find the luminous truth, the unvarying delight which is at the core of all things, the door of pain is often more direct, more immediate than that of satisfaction or contentment. . . .

Pain brings us back to a deeper truth by forcing us to concentrate in order to be able to bear, to face this thing that crushes us. It is through pain that one most easily recovers the true strength, when one is strong. It is through pain that one most easily recovers the true faith, the faith in something that is above and beyond all pain.

. . . To seek suffering and pain is a morbid attitude which must be avoided; but to run away from it out of forgetfulness, through a superficial, frivolous movement, in a spirit of diversion, is cowardice. When pain comes, it comes to teach us something. The quicker we learn it, the more the need for pain diminishes; and when we know the secret, it will no longer be possible to suffer, for that secret reveals to us the reason, the cause, the origin of suffering, and the way to pass beyond it.

The secret is to emerge from the ego, out of its prison, unite ourselves with the Divine, merge into Him, not to allow anything to separate us from Him. Then, once one has discovered this secret and realises it in one's being, pain loses its justification and suffering disappears. It is an all-powerful remedy, not only in the deeper parts of the being, in the soul, in the spiritual consciousness, but also in life and in the body.

There is no illness, no disorder that can resist if this secret is discovered and put into practice not only in the higher parts of the being, but in the cells of the body.

If one knows how to teach the cells the splendour that lies within them, if one knows how to make them understand the reality by which they exist, which gives them being, then they too enter the total harmony, and the physical disorder which caused the illness vanishes as do all other disorders of the being.

But for that, you must not be cowardly or fearful. When physical disorder attacks you, you must not be afraid, you must not run away from it; you must face it with courage, calmness, confidence, with the certitude that illness is a *falsehood* and that if you turn entirely, in full confidence, with a complete quietude to the divine Grace, It will settle in these cells as It is established in the depths of the being, and the cells themselves will share in the eternal Truth and Delight.[4]

Pain, Pleasure and the Delight of Existence

Sri Aurobindo: Pain of mind and body is a device of Nature, that is to say, of Force in her works, meant to subserve a definite transitional end in her upward evolution. The world is from the point of view of the individual a play and complex shock of multitudinous forces. In the midst of this complex play the individual stands as a limited constructed being with a limited amount of force exposed to numberless shocks which may wound, maim, break up or disintegrate the construction which he calls himself. Pain is in the nature of a nervous and physical recoil from a dangerous or harmful contact; it is a part of what the Upanishad calls *jugupsā*, the shrinking of the limited being from that which is not himself and not sympathetic or in harmony with himself, its impulse of self-defence against "others". It is, from this point of view, an indication by Nature of that which has to be avoided or, if not successfully avoided, has to be remedied. It does not come into being in the purely physical world so long as life does not enter into it; for till then mechanical methods are sufficient. Its office begins when life with its frailty and imperfect possession of Matter enters on the scene; it grows with the growth of Mind in life. Its office continues so long as Mind is bound in the life and body which it is using, dependent upon them for its knowledge and means of action, subjected to their limitations and to the egoistic impulses and aims which are born of those limitations. But if and when Mind in man becomes capable of being free, unegoistic, in harmony with all other beings and with the play of the universal forces, the use and office of suffering diminishes, its *raison d'être* must finally cease to be and it can only continue as an atavism of Nature, a habit that has survived its use, a persistence of the lower in the as yet imperfect organisation of the higher. Its eventual elimination must be an essential point in the destined conquest of the soul over subjection to Matter and egoistic limitation in Mind.

This elimination is possible because pain and pleasure themselves are currents, one imperfect, the other perverse, but still currents of the delight of existence. The reason for this imperfection and this perversion is the self-division of the being in his consciousness by measuring and limiting Maya and in consequence an egoistic and piecemeal instead of a universal reception of contacts by the individual. For the universal soul all things and all contacts of things carry in them an essence of delight best described by the Sanskrit aesthetic term, *rasa*, which means at once sap or essence of a thing and its taste. It is because we do not seek the essence of the thing in its contact with us, but look only to the manner in which it affects our desires and fears, our cravings and shrinkings that grief and pain, imperfect and transient pleasure or indifference, that is to say, blank inability to seize the essence, are the forms taken by the Rasa. If we could be entirely disinterested in mind and heart and impose that detachment on the nervous being, the progressive elimination of these imperfect and perverse forms of Rasa would be possible and the true essential taste of the inalienable delight of existence in all its variations would be within our reach.[5]

The Mother: This delight, this wonderful laughter that dissolves every shadow, every pain, every suffering! You only have to go deep enough within yourself to find the inner Sun, to let yourself be flooded by it; and then there is nothing but a cascade of harmonious, luminous, sunlit laughter, which leaves no room for any shadow or pain.

In fact, even the greatest difficulties, even the greatest sorrows, even the greatest physical pain... if you can look at them from that standpoint, from there, you see the unreality of the difficulty, the unreality of the sorrow, the unreality of the pain — and there is nothing but a joyful and luminous vibration.

In fact, this is the most powerful way of dissolving difficulties, overcoming sorrows and removing pain. The first two are relatively easy — I say relatively — the last one is more difficult because we are in the habit of considering the body and its feelings to be extremely concrete and positive; but it is the same thing, it is simply because we have not learned, we are not in the habit of regarding our body as something fluid, plastic, uncertain, malleable. We have not learned to bring into it this luminous laughter that dissolves all darkness, all difficulty, all discord, all disharmony, everything that jars, that weeps and wails.

And this Sun, this Sun of divine laughter, is at the centre of all things, the truth of all things. We must learn to see it, to feel it, to live it.[6]

References

The passages reproduced in this book have been selected from the works of Sri Aurobindo and the Mother, as identified below using the following abbreviations.

Sri Aurobindo:
Complete Works of Sri Aurobindo (CWSA)
Sri Aurobindo Birth Centenary Library (SABCL)
Evening Talks, 1982 ed. (ET)
Correspondence with Sri Aurobindo, 1983-84 ed. (CSA)
Guidance from Sri Aurobindo, Vol. I, 1974; Vol. II, 1976; Vol. III, 1987 (GSA)
Talks with Sri Aurobindo, 2001 ed. (TSA)
Mother India (MI)
Unpublished letters (UP letter)

The Mother:
Collected Works of the Mother, Vols. 3-9, 11 (identified as "Talk of [date]")
Collected Works of the Mother, Vols. 10, 13-17 (CWM)
Bulletin of Sri Aurobindo International Centre of Education (Bulletin)
White Roses, 1999 ed. (Copyright Huta) (WR)
Talks not published by Sri Aurobindo Ashram (identified with an asterisk as "*Talk of [date]")
Unpublished letters (UP letter)

INTRODUCTION
1 Bulletin 24:2, 28-29
2 Talk of 19.3.1958
3 CWSA 23:5-8, 45-47
4 Talk of 7.4.1929
5 Talk of 7.10.1964
6 SABCL 26:208
7 SABCL 23:505
8 SABCL 24:1220
9 SABCL 19:987-88
10 SABCL 22:340
11 CWM 15:315

12 Talk of 7.10.1964
13 Talk of 16.6.1929
14 *Talk of 25.1.1967
15 *Talk of 8.2.1967
16 Talk of 22.7.1953
17 Talk of 19.5.1929
18 Talk of 22.7.1953

PART I: PSYCHOLOGICAL
CAUSES OF ILLNESS
1 CWM 15:149
2 Talk of 16.6.1929

3 Talk of 16.6.1929
4 Talk of 24.6.1953
5 CWM 16:323-24
6 *Talk of 26.9.1964
7 Talk of 22.7.1953
8 Talk of 16.6.1929
9 SABCL 24:1564
10 CSA 737-39
11 SABCL 22:350
12 SABCL 24:1564-65
13 Talk of 11.5.1955
14 Talk of 31.3.1951
15 Talk of 27.1.1951
16 Talk of 2.4.1951
17 SABCL 24:1572
18 UP letter
19 Talk of 23.12.1953
20 Talk of 7.10.1953
21 *Talk of 25.10.1960
22 *Talk of 20.6.1962
23 *Talk of 30.6.1965
24 CWM 15:151
25 CWM 15:156
26 CWM 14:262
27 Talk of 11.5.1955
28 Talk of 19.6.1957
29 Talk of 22.7.1953
30 Talk of 14.3.1951
31 Talk of 19.5.1929
32 Talk of 22.7.1953
33 Talk of 14.10.1953
34 Talk of 14.3.1951
35 SABCL 22:353
36 SABCL 24:1596
37 Talk of 11.5.1955
38 Talk of 13.10.1954
39 CSA 1054
40 CWM 14:389

PART II: CURE BY INNER
MEANS
1 Talk of 5.2.1951
2 SABCL 24:1569
3 SABCL 24:1563
4 ET 29
5 SABCL 24:1567
6 GSA 1:214
7 SABCL 24:1602-3
8 CWM 15:158
9 *Talk of 14.10.1964
10 ET 178-79
11 SABCL 23:664
12 CWM 15:158
13 CWM 12:22
14 Talk of 5.2.1951
15 Talk of 27.8.1958
16 Talk of 5.1.1955
17 SABCL 24:1570
18 SABCL 24:1589
19 SABCL 24:1106
20 ET 179
21 Talk of 19.6.1957
22 Talk of 5.5.1929
23 SABCL 23:577-78
24 SABCL 24:1567
25 CWSA 23:343-47
26 CWSA 13:529-30
27 CWM 15:156-57
28 Talk of 27.4.1955
29 CWM 17:63-64
30 CWM 17:92
31 UP letter
32 CWM 10:171
33 Talk of 20.1.1951
34 SABCL 24:1394
35 Talk of 17.11.1954
36 Talk of 11.5.1955
37 Talk of 27.4.1955
38 Talk of 8.9.1954

39 Talk of 29.8.1956
40 Talk of 8.7.1953
41 Talk of 29.9.1954
42 CWM 15:163
43 CWM 16:195
44 CWM 17:195
45 UP letter
46 Talk of 17.10.1956
47 Talk of 8.9.1954
48 Talk of 12.1.1965
49 Talk of 23.6.1929
50 Talk of 5.4.1951
51 CWM 10:145
52 CWM 15:161
53 WR 76
54 CWM 15:163
55 TSA 1:12
56 Talk of 26.12.1956
57 Talk of 22.10.1958
58 CWM 17:193
59 SABCL 18:85-86
60 SABCL 22:234
61 SABCL 22:235-36
62 *Talk of 2.10.1961
63 Talk of 9.12.1953
64 Talk of 20.1.1951
65 SABCL 22:294
66 SABCL 18:104-5
67 Talk of 26.9.1956
68 SABCL 23:738-39
69 SABCL 24:1457
70 ET 29
71 Talk of 29.6.1955
72 Talk of 23.12.1953
73 Talk of 26.12.1956
74 Talk of 31.7.1957
75 Talk of 24.3.1951
76 Talk of 12.2.1951
77 Talk of 7.4.1929
78 Talk of 4.1.1951

79 Talk of 9.4.1958
80 *Talk of 7.8.1963
81 SABCL 22:347
82 GSA 2:9
83 SABCL 24:1432
84 SABCL 22:323-24
85 CWM 15:171
86 CWM 15:159
87 Talk of 7.10.1953
88 Talk of 7.10.1953
89 Talk of 25.1.1951
90 CWM 12:7
91 Talk of 19.5.1954
92 Talk of 31.7.1957
93 Talk of 31.7.1957
94 *Talk of 8.2.1967
95 *Talk of 18.3.1970
96 Talk of 23.11.1968
97 *Talk of 16.10.1971
98 *Talk of 14.5.1964
99 Talk of 4.7.1956

PART III: CURE BY SPIRITUAL FORCE
1 SABCL 24:1563
2 Talk of 23.6.1929
3 CWM 16:185
4 CWM 10:192
5 SABCL 23:609-10
6 TSA 1:8-9
7 CWM 14:91
8 CWM 10:323
9 CWM 16:195
10 CWM 17:196
11 CWM 15:169
12 CWM 15:172
13 CWM 10:290
14 Talk of June, 1931
15 SABCL 23:581
16 CWM 15:341

17 Talk of 9.7.1958
18 Talk of 3.10.1956
19 CWM 14:95
20 CWM 17:189
21 SABCL 22:174
22 CWSA 24:621
23 Talk of 1.8.1956
24 Talk of 29.10.1958
25 SABCL 24:1150
26 GSA 1:189
27 SABCL 22:318
28 SABCL 22:216-18
29 CSA 128-30
30 Talk of 20.5.1953
31 SABCL 22:218-19
32 SABCL 25:144
33 Talk of 16.6.1929
34 Talk of 16.9.1953
35 MI 11:12, 13
36 CWM 15:160
37 CWM 15:176
38 SABCL 23:637
39 SABCL 23:582
40 SABCL 24:1581
41 SABCL 24:1722
42 Talk of 31.3.1951
43 Talk of 31.3.1951
44 SABCL 24:1678
45 SABCL 25:147
46 SABCL 24:1576-77
47 SABCL 24:1580
48 SABCL 24:1577
49 SABCL 24:1678
50 SABCL 24:1567
51 ET 167
52 SABCL 24:1187
53 Talk of 21.4.1954
54 MI 21:5, 348
55 CSA 517-18
56 MI 21:5, 348

57 GSA 3:128
58 CWM 16:425
59 Talk of 7.10.1964
60 Talk of 30.3.1955
61 Talk of 7.10.1964
62 SABCL 24:1689-90
63 SABCL 23:604-5
64 Talk of 18.11.1953
65 CWM 15:164
66 Talk of 20.5.1953
67 Talk of 17.11.1954
68 Talk of 16.12.1953
69 Talk of 3.6.1953
70 CWM 15:161
71 CWM 15:162
72 WR 186
73 *Talk of 20.6.1970
74 Talk of 24.3.1965
75 Talk of 16.10.1971

PART IV: MEDICINE AND
HEALING
1 SABCL 24:1569
2 Talk of 19.6.1957
3 UP letter
4 SABCL 24:1568
5 SABCL 24:1570
6 SABCL 25:353-54
7 CWM 15:170
8 UP letter
9 UP letter
10 CWM 10:325
11 SABCL 26:214-15
12 TSA 1:43
13 ET 202
14 CSA 696
15 CSA 428
16 CWM 15:170
17 UP letter
18 CSA 446

19 UP letter
20 CWM 12:15
21 *Talk of 4.12.1965
22 CWM 17:195
23 CWM 15:172
24 CWSA 12:477
25 CWSA 12:475
26 CWSA 12:474
27 CWSA 12:476
28 CWSA 12:477
29 CWSA 12:477
30 CWM 10:327
31 CWM 10:327
32 *Talk of 13.11.1965
33 *Talk of 4.8.1965
34 *Talk of 19.5.1965
35 *Talk of 26.9.1964
36 TSA 1:147-48
37 SABCL 24:1588
38 CWM 15:169
39 CWM 17:403
40 CWM 17:192
41 CWM 15:167
42 CSA 570
43 CWM 15:167
44 CWM 15:167-68
45 SABCL 24:1568-69
46 SABCL 24:1573
47 CSA 121
48 UP letter
49 CSA 337
50 CSA 213
51 CSA 422
52 CSA 384
53 GSA 1:245
54 GSA 1:246-47
55 CSA 429
56 CSA 568-69
57 CSA 571
58 SABCL 26:210-11
59 SABCL 26:211-12
60 SABCL 26:203-5
61 CSA 1129
62 CSA 812
63 ET 212
64 CWM 15:177
65 MI 28:2, 106
66 SABCL 24:1585
67 SABCL 26:475
68 *Talk of 19.5.1965
69 Talk of 19.6.1957
70 SABCL 25:376-77
71 CSA 200-1
72 CSA 420
73 CSA 424-25
74 TSA 1:28
75 SABCL 22:264
76 TSA 1:46
77 SABCL 22:480
78 CWSA 23:480
79 Talk of 23.7.1958
80 CSA 819, 822
81 GSA 3:247
82 CWM 17:193
83 *Talk of 26.9.1964
84 CWM 16:429
85 CWM 16:19
86 SABCL 22:220
87 SABCL 22:481
88 SABCL 22:480
89 Talk of 31.3.1951
90 CWM 15:166
91 CWM 17:407-8
92 *Talk of 13.12.1969
93 TSA 1:4
94 *Talk of 20.9.1969
95 *Talk of 13.4.1966
96 Talk of 8.1.1958
97 SABCL 23:831
98 SABCL 23:838-39

99 SABCL 24:1490
100 Talk of 1.7.1953
101 Talk of 8.8.1956

CONCLUSION
  1 SABCL 28:171
  2 Talk of 28.9.1966
  3 Talk of 23.4.1951

4 Talk of 13.2.1957
5 SABCL 18:107-8
6 CWM 10:158

BACK COVER
  1 CSA 1054
  2 Talk of 13.2.1957

Glossary

This glossary includes mainly (1) Sanskrit words that are not defined where they occur in the text and (2) English terms with a special significance in the works from which this book has been compiled. The definitions are meant to explain these words only in contexts in which they appear in this book. Words printed in **bold** type in the definitions are themselves defined in the glossary.

ādhāra (Adhara, Adhar) — vessel; the physical, **vital** and **mental** system as a vehicle of the consciousness and force of the **Spirit**.

adverse forces — forces of the **vital world** that oppose the higher movement of **evolution** and are agents of disharmony in human life at its present stage; also referred to as hostile or anti-divine forces.

Ananda — bliss; the unvarying delight which is at the core of all things.

anti-divine forces — see **adverse forces**.

Ayurveda — the ancient Vedic system of Indian medicine.

body-consciousness — the consciousness that belongs to the body and is concerned with its functionings. It is a part of the **physical consciousness**, below the level of the **physical mind** and largely **subconscient**, but possessing an instinctive knowledge.

Brahmic consciousness — awareness of the eternal Reality (*brahman*) that is expressed in the universe.

Chakras — the seven centres of consciousness in the **subtle body**, connecting the **subliminal** being on its various levels with the outer personality.

dharmasādhana — the means of fulfilment of *dharma*, defined by Sri Aurobindo as "the inner and the outer law by which the divine Will and Wisdom work out the spiritual evolution of mankind".

Divine Force — see **spiritual force**.

evolution — the progressive manifestation of consciousness in matter. Having reached the human level, its next step according to Sri Aurobindo will be to go beyond mind to **Supermind** and reveal the **Spirit** integrally in life.

Force — see **spiritual force**.

gnostic — pertaining to the gnosis or spiritual knowledge beyond mind, especially on the plane of **Supermind**.

Grace — the free and irresistible action of the **Spirit** working for the best in all circumstances with the power to override the mechanical determinism of cosmic laws.

Guru — a spiritual guide; a teacher of any branch of ancient knowledge in the Indian tradition.

Hakimi — a Muslim system of medicine, also called Unani.

Higher Mind — the luminous thought-mind that is the first of several planes of consciousness between ordinary mind and **Supermind**. On all of these planes, according to Sri Aurobindo, "the realisation of the One is the natural basis of consciousness"; but on the higher planes, "the vision of the workings of the One becomes ever wider and is attended with a greater instrumentality of Force".

hostile forces — see **adverse forces**.

inconscience, the inconscient—the negation of consciousness from which **evolution** in this world began. Until it is transformed by **Supermind**, it persists as the cause of the inability of matter to embody the truth and immortality of the **Spirit**.

Integral Yoga — a form of **Yoga** that seeks to manifest the **Spirit** in life and matter by effectuating a **transformation** in all parts of our nature.

intuition — a faculty of direct perception derived from knowledge by identity and not dependent on reasoning. Intuition at its highest, in Sri Aurobindo's terminology, is the plane of consciousness just below **Overmind** and can be experienced only at an advanced stage of **Yoga**. What is usually called intuition is diluted and mixed with inferior **mental** or **vital** movements (mental intuition, vital intuition) or else an imitation (false intuition).

jugupsā — repulsion; self-protecting recoil.

Karma — the sum of one's actions, each action being viewed as a link in a chain of cause and effect extending over many lives.

Kundalini Shakti — the latent power asleep in the lowest of the **Chakras**, where in the Indian tradition it is described as coiled up like a snake.

Maya — the power of consciousness to shape finite appearances out of infinite existence.

Medea — a sorceress in Greek mythology, in whose cauldron Aeson was rejuvenated and Pelias perished.

mental — pertaining to mind, the faculty of thought and intelligence, which is the instrument of a kind of cognition where the subject is separate from the object; an intermediate range of the spectrum of consciousness which has found expression in the human stage of **evolution**.

mental world — a supraphysical plane of existence governed by the mental principle.

nervous — see vital-physical.

nervous envelope — a vital-physical aura that surrounds and protects the body.

overmental — belonging to the Overmind.

Overmind — a plane of cosmic consciousness just below Supermind. Overmind differs from Supermind in that, although it knows the infinite unity, it subordinates it to the play of multiplicity. Due to this limitation, its power is ultimately insufficient for the transformation that is the object of Integral Yoga.

physical consciousness — the consciousness in the body (sometimes including the subtle body).

physical mind — the part of the physical consciousness that gives mental form to physical experience.

psychic — pertaining to the soul; the inmost being which is normally hidden from us in the depths of our subliminal consciousness. It supports our evolution from life to life and is the key to the possibility of transformation.

Purusha — the inner conscious being, experienced as distinct from the outer nature, whose movements it witnesses and upholds.

rajasic — dominated by rajas, the kinetic and turbulent mode of energy which is characteristic of the vital part of the nature (cf. tamasic and sattwic).

rasa — sap, juice; essence; taste; the essence of delight in all things.

Sadhak — one who seeks spiritual realisation by Sadhana.

Sadhana — spiritual discipline; practice of Yoga.

sadhu — a holy man; an ascetic.

Sat — existence in its unconditioned purity, timeless, spaceless, formless and indivisible.

sattwic — dominated by sattva, the harmonising and intelligent mode of energy which is proper to the mental part of the nature (cf. tamasic and rajasic).

Shastra — the systematic formulation of any aspect of the science and art of life.

soul — see psychic.

Spirit — the one Self of all, whose nature is immortal existence, consciousness, force and bliss. Although it has concealed itself behind the appearances of the material world, it is the source of all things and is present everywhere. It can be experienced through Yoga and embodied in life through an integral **transformation**.

spiritual force — the power of the **Spirit**; in the **Integral Yoga** it may descend from any plane of spiritual consciousness from **Higher Mind** upwards.

subconscient, subconscious — below the level of normal conscious awareness; an obscure and incoherent part of the being which borders on **inconscience** and exerts a powerful influence on the body.

subliminal — behind the outer consciousness; the inner being. According to Sri Aurobindo, it has "a consciousness much wider, more luminous, more in possession of itself and things than that which wakes upon our surface".

subtle body — a body made of **subtle physical** substance, forming part of the **subliminal** being and supporting the gross (physical) body.

subtle physical — belonging to the lowest of the immaterial planes of existence, that which resembles most closely the physical world in which we live, but is beyond the range of the outward senses.

Supermind — the plane of consciousness on which the limits of mind (including the spiritual mind-planes from **Higher Mind** to **Overmind**) are entirely transcended; its nature is a knowledge of infinite unity expressing itself in an infinite multiplicity.

supramental — belonging to the **Supermind**.

supraphysical — not perceptible to the physical senses or physical instruments, but capable of being known by faculties that can be developed through **Yoga**.

tamas — see **tamasic**.

tamasic—dominated by *tamas*, the inert and unintelligent mode of energy which is characteristic of the physical part of the nature (cf. **rajasic** and **sattwic**).

Tantras — the texts of a particular system of **Yoga**, in which the **Kundalini Shakti** is awakened by specific processes and ascends through the **Chakras**.

transformation — radical change in the inner and outer nature in all its parts, brought about progressively in **Integral Yoga** by the action of forces belonging to higher and higher planes of consciousness up to **Supermind**.

Upanishad — any of a class of ancient Sanskrit texts regarded as the source of the Vedanta philosophy.

vital — pertaining to the life-force; the part of our nature that links the **mental** and the physical. Its essential function is enjoyment and possession; its energies are necessary for the fullness of our embodied existence, but can be the cause of many disturbances until they are purified and transformed by **Yoga**.

vital mind — the part of the consciousness that gives **mental** form to **vital** movements such as impulses, desires and emotions.

vital-physical — pertaining to the part of the life-force that is involved in the states and activities of the body (sometimes including the **subtle body**).

vital world — a **supraphysical** plane of existence governed by the **vital** principle.

Yoga — literally, union; any of various methods of transcending the normal limits of human nature and entering into contact and union with a higher consciousness and greater reality. In this book, the word usually refers to the **Integral Yoga** developed by Sri Aurobindo and the Mother.

Yoga-Shakti — the **spiritual force** activated by the practice of **Yoga**.

Yogi (also **Yogin**) — one who practises **Yoga**; one who has achieved the self-mastery or spiritual realisation sought through any form of Yoga.

Yogic force — see **spiritual force**.

Yogin — see **Yogi**.

Index

A

Accidents
    attitude and, 49-50, 131, 191
    attracted by fear, 30-31, 63-64
    causes of, 25-28, 46-47
    Force protects against, 17
    forces behind, 31-32
    moment of choice in, 117-18
    nervous envelope and, 46-47
Allopathy, 116, 186-87
Anaemia
    moving in the sun for, 188
Ananda
    bringing, into the body, 12, 108,
        125, 157, 172
    behind pain, 169, 231
Aspiration
    in the body and cells, 129-30,
        178
    for capacity to heal, 217
    certitude in, 174-75
    for change of consciousness,
        122-23, 148, 155, 172
    for cure of others, 198
    for the Divine, 138, 143, 172-
        74, 225, 229-32
    intensity of, 122-23, 176, 229
    and passive receptivity, 106-7,
        166-67, 175
    psychic, always answered, 175-
        76
    in suffering, 162, 229-32
    and surrender, 178
    See also Prayer
Aura, 41; see also Nervous enve-
    lope

Auto-suggestion
    Coué and, 80-83
    cure by, 48-53, 126, 201
    defined, 82
    subconscient and, 82
    See also Mental (thought) for-
        mations
Ayurveda, 186-87, 212

B

Body
    bringing peace into, 107-8
    can cure itself, 36, 49-50, 129-
        32, 183
    capacity to endure pain in, 94
    changing the habits of, 88-90
    consciousness of, 12, 125-27
    consents to illness, 76, 83
    detaching the mind from, 87
    disequilibrium and illness in, 21-
        30 passim
    divinity of, 54, 132, 136
    going out of, 98-99, 162-63
    increasing the receptivity of,
        160-62
    an instrument of the Spirit, 11,
        12, 91, 167
    mastery over, 84-85, 89-91, 232
    memory in, 70
    mistreated by mind and vital,
        128-29
    opening to the Force, 141-42,
        164-66
    power of thought over, 48-53
    precariousness of health in, 91
    resistances in, 158, 185

shrinks from pain, 178
subconscient and, 67-71
subconscient fear in, 54-56, 64
sure instinct of, 128, 131
surrendering, 176-78
See also Body-consciousness;
  Body-mind
Body-consciousness
accepts illness, 48, 87
changing its reaction to illness,
  87
defined, 13, 125-27
opening to the Force, 160, 164-
  67
resistance in, 13, 168
See also Body; Body-mind
Body-mind
chief obstacle to transformation,
  13
conversion of, 13
a tangible truth, 13
See also Body; Body-consciousness
Brahmic consciousness, 50-51
Breathing
to calm the heart, 29

C

Calm
bringing, into pain, 94
inner, for change of consciousness, 120
necessary for cure, 77,103-5,
  163, 233
to relieve tension, 162
the supreme, 229
See also Peace; Quiet, quietude
Cancer, 206-7
wrong habit of the cells, 206

See also Cyst
Cells
aspiration and surrender of,
  129, 174, 178
awakening consciousness in,
  108, 134
awakening faith in, 86, 132
becoming conscious of the Divine, 72, 111, 136, 138, 160,
  178, 233
consciousness of, 12, 13, 129
fear in, 55-58, 61, 66, 158
illness, a wrong habit in, 52,
  133, 206
peace in, 108, 115
response of, to illness, 170, 192-
  93
shrink from pain, 178
waking the will to conquer in,
  77, 52-53
Chakras, 152
Children
have confidence in life, 50, 174
Cholera, 39, 41, 59, 62
Cold, cough, 26, 40, 42, 49, 132-
  33
vibratory process of a, 132-34
Congestion, 87, 99, 162
Consciousness
accidents and an awakened, 47,
  117-19
change of, 3, 83, 109-10, 112,
  119-24, 135
consents to illness, 79, 87, 169,
  defined, 110-11
and illness, 35, 106-7, 111, 141,
  160, 209, 215, 219
inner and outer, and illness, 15-
  16, 21, 87, 113-14
mastery over one's, 73, 79

placing one's, 92, 111, 112-15,
134-35
planes and parts of, 67-69, 111,
125-27, 218
widening the, 100-102, 161
Coué
auto-suggestion and, 80-85
secret of his method, 82
Cyst
wrong habit of the cells, 52-53
See also Cancer

D

Death
reason for, 16, 23
Depression, 89, 130, 152, 164
lowers resistance to illness, 18,
39, 56
Determinism
freedom and, 176
Diagnosis
and intuition, 209-14
Digestion
quietude for good, 105, 177
Disease, disorders, *see* Illness
Disequilibrium
accidents and, 46-47
illness and, 18, 21-30, 127
See also Illness, causes of
Divine, the
action of, 141-42, 154
all is the Divine, 112, 179, 200
aspiration for, 143, 173-74, 225,
229-30
convincing the body and cells of,
54, 72, 108, 136-38, 178-79,
233
doctor as an instrument of, 198-
203

faith in, 142, 145-49
idea of, 10
identification and surrender to,
8, 111-14, 134-35, 143, 153,
176-79
leaving result to, 141
only, can heal, 142
trust in, and fear, 64-66
union with, an all-powerful remedy, 190, 230, 233
Divine Consciousness
descent of, into body, 12, 68, 72,
138, 172
human consciousness and, 11,
218
identification with, 145, 155,
218
Divine Grace
action of, 144, 149-51
calling the, 148-49, 172-73, 225
cure of illness and, 141-45, 185,
196, 197, 232-33
defined, 4, 143, 149-50
faith in, 145-48, 169, 224-25,
232
and illness as a means of progress, 19, 147
intervention of, 149-51, 172-73,
224-25, 230
letting it work, 144-45
miracles of, 148-49
reliance on, 148-49, 197
resistance to the working of, 151
surrender to, 138, 142, 225
Divine Influence/Presence
faith in, 147
freedom from fear and, 66
governing the functions of the
body, 72
living in, for relief of suffering,

94, 113-14, 135-36
opening to, 172, 190
Divine Love
intervention of Grace in, 230
Doctor(s)
chief role of, 196
choosing one's, 185, 195-96
crystallize illness, 193
diseases and, 191-92
healing power necessary in, 195
as instruments of the Divine,
193-94, 197-203
and intuitive diagnosis, 209-14
patient's faith in, 189, 195
qualities of, 195-98, 201-2
telling the truth to patients, 215-
16

E

Ego, egoism
emerging from, 102, 233-34
fear and, 65
surrender of, in Yoga, 8
veils the Divine, 200
Epidemics
caused by fear, 58
confidence in vaccination and,
59
flu epidemic in Japan, 32-35
forces behind, 34, 41, 59
immunity from, 57, 62
not necessarily contagious, 137
Equilibrium,
all is a question of, 21-30 *passim*
of the body, 127
establishing, in illness, 24
illness is a break in, 17, 26
mind and vital disturb, 127-29

resistance to illness and, 46, 56
restoring the, 35-38
triple, 27
Etheric body, *see* Nervous envelope
Evolution
body's resistance to, 1
compression of, by yoga, 6
moment of transition in, 1
struggle of forces in, 3-4
Eyes
weakness of, 115

F

Faith
of the body and cells, 84-86, 94,
132, 164
cure by, 152, 189, 207, 220,
in the Divine, 142, 145-50, 159-
60, 189, 224-25, 232
effective and ineffective, 147-48,
174, 198
imagination and, 80-82
immunity and, 39, 62
medicines and, 108, 184-86,
189-90
never lose hope or, 145
psychic and integral, 85, 146
yoga and, 17, 172
Fatigue
attitude towards, 87, 89, 90
causes of, 128
minimising, 12
nervous envelope and, 46, 56
Fear
attracts what it is afraid of, 63
contagion, epidemics and, 33,
56-58, 64
formation of, and pain, 92

is lack of trust in the Divine, 54,
  65-66
mental, vital, physical, 56-58, 61
reasons for, 65-66
remedy for, 63-64
role of, in illness, 41, 130, 190,
  223
subconscient, 54-55, 64,
Fever, 14, 29, 33-34, 36, 40, 42,
  58, 98, 153, 162
septic, 50
typhoid, 163
Flu, *see* Influenza, flu
Food
  attitude to, 88
  calling peace before eating, 105.
  psychic knowledge and, 116
Force (divine, spiritual)
  action of, 11-12, 199, 202-5,
    217-19
  applying, from outside the body,
    162-63
  aspiring for, 172-76
  becoming conscious of, 155-57
  defined, 152-57, 204-5
  does not succeed in all cases, 153
  Earth not ready for, 158
  in healing, 11, 37-38, 41, 140-
    42, 153-54, 184-85, 197-208
    passim, 217-21 *passim*
  medicine as support for, 181,
    183-86, 197-200
  opening the physical conscious-
    ness to, 136-37, 164-65
  receptivity to, 158-60, 165-67
  resistance to, 1, 158-59, 168-69
  surrendering to, 177-79
  yogic force and, 154
  See also Receptivity
Force, the Mother's

opening to, 152, 157, 164
resistance to, 168
Forces, adverse
  evolution and, 4
  illness and, 32, 37, 39-44, 169,
    207
  unconsciousness attracts, 9
Forces, universal
  all life is a play of, 152
  man and, 15, 152, 234

G

Germs, microbes
  illness and, 18, 24, 30, 50, 61
  origin of, 32-33, 40-41, 43, 59
  that cure, 59-60
God
  and Nature, 7-8, 41
  treats his friends severely, 231

H

Habits
  chronic illnesses are, 52
  origin of, 52
Hair-loss
  cured by positive formations, 81
Hakimi [Unani], 186
Headache, 26, 99, 122, 159, 161
Healing
  capacity for, 195, 197, 217
  by faith in the cells, 86
  with the hands, 220-22
  imagination and, 85
  knowledge and, 95
  Mother's experience of, 132-34
  Mother's Force and, 152
  Sri Aurobindo's power of, 222
  See also Illness, cure of

Health, natural
a mighty force, 189
Higher Mind, 154
Homeopathy, 116, 186
practice of, 200-201
principle of, 186-87
Hospitals
mental atmosphere of, 192

I

Illness
acceptance of, 48, 69-70, 76, 78, 93
cherishing, 36, 130, 205
collaboration of patient in, 203, 205-6
falsehood of, 111, 191, 233
imaginary, 24, 93
intensity of aspiration in, 229-30
moral condition in, 62-63
no incurable, 28, 145, 207
no two cases identical, 191, 209
as an opportunity for growth, 19, 110, 112, 216, 220, 231-33
passivity and inertia in, 165-67
pay no attention to, 87, 93-95, 134-35, 137
psychic being and, 113-17
refusing, 55-56
role of suggestion in, 39, 56, 60, 75, 131, 149, 203-4, 207; *see also* Auto-suggestion; Mental (thought) formations
vibrations and, 30, 43-44, 51, 56, 111-12, 142, 221
vibratory mode of, 16, 59-60, 132-34, 191

wrong habit of the body, 26, 52-53, 67-69, 83, 87, 90, 139, 164, 184, 206
in Yoga, 14-19
Illness, causes of
attacks of adverse forces, 31-32, 37, 39, 42, 169
depression, 18, 39, 56, 160
disequilibrium of the being, 14-47 *passim*, 95, 127
doubt in the cells, 53, 77, 136
external, 30-35
falsity of consciousness, 111-12
fear, 33, 41, 54-58, 61-66, 92, 94
internal, 28-30
psychological, 21-72 *passim*
resistance to transformation, 1, 14-16, 23, 133, 159, 177, 193, 231
subconscient, 40-42, 54, 67-72, 82, 168, 185
universal forces, 15, 152
wrong thinking, 48-50
Illness, cure of
auto-suggestion, 48-50, 52-53, 56, 80-83, 126, 132-33, 201
calm and peace, *see* Calm; Peace; Quiet, quietude
changing one's consciousness, 109, 111-17, *see also* Consciousness
decision of body, 36, 126-27, 183
erasing the body memory, 70-71
opening to the Divine, *see* Divine, the; Divine Grace, etc.
opening to the Force, *see* Force (divine, spiritual); Force, the Mother's

patience for, 93-94, 170-71, 177
perseverance, persistence for, 53,
    75, 170
receptivity to the Force, *see* Re-
    ceptivity
removing psychological element,
    71, 95-96
restoring the equilibrium, 24-26,
    36, 142
sincerity and, 78-79
three steps for, 137-38
trust in life and, 49
two ways for, 219
union with the Divine, 1, 233
use of knowledge and reason in,
    95
use of medicine, *see* Medicine
using the will, *see* Will; Will
    (divine)
Illnesses and disorders
anaemia, 188
cancer, 206-7
cholera, 39, 41, 59, 62
cold, cough, 26, 40, 42, 49, 132-
    33
congestion, 87, 99, 162
cyst, 52-53
depression, 18, 39, 56, 89, 130,
    152, 164
digestion, 105, 177
epidemics, 32-35, 41, 57-59, 62,
    137
eyes, weakness of, 115
fatigue, 12, 46, 56, 87, 89, 90,
    126, 128
fever, 14, 29, 33-34, 36, 40, 42,
    50, 58, 98, 153, 162-63
hair, falling, 81
headache, 26, 99, 122, 159, 161
influenza, flu, 32, 41, 43

insanity, 14, 90, 204
nervous disorders, 26, 31, 93,
    162, 165, 204
plague, 39, 41
skin diseases, 23
stomach pains, 115
sunstroke, 99, 162-63
tetanus, 50
toothache, teeth, 23, 26, 97,
    134, 221
Imagination
Coué's method and, 80-83, 85
a power of formation, 80-81
See also Auto-suggestion
Immunity
absolute, 42-43, 71
equilibrium and, 27, 46
faith and, 62
See also Nervous envelope
Inconscient
body memory and, 70
process of a cold and, 132
Inertia
of the body, 15, 125, 139, 229
getting rid of, 75, 125, 229
passivity and, 165
Influenza, flu, 32, 41, 43
Inner being, *see* Consciousness,
    inner and outer; Psychic being
Insanity, 14, 90, 204
Intuition
developing the, 91, 212-214
doctors and, 196,199, 201, 209-
    11
the psychic and, 146

K

Karma, 89,143
Kaviraji [Ayurveda], *see* Ayurveda

Kundalini Shakti, 152

M

Material plane/consciousness
  influence of, in illness, 82, 149,
    170, 184
  resistance to the Force, 14-15,
    23, 158, 169-70, 185
Matter
  awakening consciousness in, 11
  the difficulty of, 169
  ignorance, inertia in, 229
  infusion of a new principle in,
    1, 3
  mind in, 169
  resistance to divine Influence in,
    16
  true nature of, 11, 13-14
Medical Science
  illness and, 1, 18, 45, 191-92
  and self-cure, 190
Medical systems
  act as channels for the Force,
    186
  Allopathy, 116, 186-87
  Ayurveda, 186-87, 212
  Hakimi [Unani], 186
  Homeopathy, 116, 186-87, 200-
    201
  Naturopathy, 186
  Osteopathy, 186
Medicine(s), drugs
  consciousness more powerful
    than, 35, 119
  cure without, 33-34, 49, 83-84,
    145, 153, 188-89
  doctor's atmosphere and, 195,
    200-201
  faith in, 108, 183-86, 189

fashionable, 188
indispensable in ordinary life, 60
natural resistance undermined
  by, 189
are palliatives, 71
reliance on, 189-90
side effects of, 183, 187-88
use of the Force and, 152, 170,
  181, 184-85, 190, 197, 199-
  200, 203
use of will and, 77
Meditation, 106
Mental (thought) formations
  a cold and, 132-33
  giving dynamism to, 84, 117,
    138, 224
  to help and protect others, 222-
    25
  illness and, 28, 43, 48-50, 69-
    70, 220
  power of, 50-51, 80-82, 141,
    223
  undoing wrong, 71
  See also Auto-suggestion
Mental quietude/silence
  cure and, 103-4, 107, 159-60,
    222-23
  establishing, 103-106, 130
  intuition and, 212-14
  meditation and, 106-7
  receptivity to the Force and,
    159, 172, 222-23
  See also Peace; Quiet, quietude
Mind, mental being
  attitude of, in pain, 97, 107-8,
    164, 232
  of the body, 13; *see also* Body-
    mind
  consciousness and, 111, 125
  detaching, from the body, 87-89

disequilibrium of, 14, 17, 24, 27, 128
fear in, 58, 61; *see also* Fear
illness and, 24, 27, 48-50, 84, 93, 177, 190
mastery of, over body, 89-91, 126-29
in Matter, 169; *see also* Matter
and the subconscient, 67-71; *see also* Subconscient
See also Physical Mind; Vital mind
Miracles
an awakened consciousness and, 119
Divine Grace and, 148-49
Sri Aurobindo does not deal in, 153-54
Mother, the
force of, 152, 157, 164
healing with her hand, 220-21
praying to, in illness, 173
Mother's experiences
a cold and an extraordinary healing power, 132-34
difficulty of the material mind, 169
disorder or illness?, 192-93
domain where "disease" and "cure" no longer exist, 193-94
mastery of physical suffering, 178-79
"no doctor, no doctor", 193
shift in consciousness, 134

N

Nature
an all-round healer, 189

and evolution, 3, 5-7, 208, 233-34
habits of, 88-90
and illness, 76, 210
living in harmony with, 114
medical systems and, 186
never repeats itself, 209
pain a device of, 233
Nervous disorders, 26, 31, 93, 162, 165, 204
Naturopathy, 186
Nervous envelope
defined, 39
illness and, 39-47, 56
immunity and, 39-47
protection against accidents, 46-47
psychological states and, 39, 46
Neuralgic pains, 26

O

Osteopathy, 186
Overmind, 154

P

Pain
action of the Force on, 164-65, 168-69
control over, 80, 95-97, 137-38
defined, 234
finding the truth in, 232-33
going out of the body and, 98-99
healing, with the hands, 220-22
mental factor in, 94-95
pleasure and, 232-63
receptivity of the body and, 160-62

shifting the consciousness and, 92-93, 100, 134-35, 152
Passivity
  for cure, 100, 206
  the Force and, 155, 166
  inertia and, 147, 165-67
Patient
  attitude of, for cure, 205-7
  faith of, 186, 189
  power of thought around, 198, 203, 223
  preoccupied with illness, 205-6, 220
  telling the truth to, 215-16
Peace
  as basis for life, 4
  bringing, into disharmony, 25, 36
  in the cells and body, 55-56, 107-8, 125, 138
  in illness, 103, 107-8, 115
  in the mind, 103-6
  psychic being and, 115
  for relief of tension, 161
  the supreme, 229
  See also Calm; Quiet, quietude
Physical consciousness
  accepts illness, 48
  inner or subtle, 42, 67, 91
  opening to the Force, 136-37, 165, 172
  See also Body-consciousness
Physical mind
  attitude of, 168
  bringing peace into, 106, 115
  mastery over, 51
  nature of, 91, 126, 157
  rejecting illness with, 48
Plague, 39, 41
Prayer

aspiration, call and, 172, 174-76
  formulating one's, 225
  to help and protect others, 223-25
  to the Mother, 173
  psychic, always answered, 175-76
Prognostications
  harm done by, 149, 214-15
Psychic being, soul
  above all suffering, 113-15
  bringing, into the physical, 115
  contact with, 115-17, 120-22, 129
  defined, 113
  faith and, 146
  finding the, 122-24
  living in, 111, 113-15
  peace and, 115, 138
  true knowledge in, 115-17, 146
  has trust, 175
Purusha
  attitude of mind towards body, 88-89
  mental, as master of Nature, 89-91

Q

Quiet, quietude
  aspiration and, 175-76
  bringing, into body, 36, 55-56, 160, 177
  digestion and, 105, 177
  to receive the Force, 159-60, 164, 166, 172, 222-23
  mental, *see* Mental quietude/silence
  necessary for cure, 53, 78, 93-

94, 138, 164, 233
a positive state, 104
receptivity and, 159-60
in vibration of nervous envelope,
43-44
See also Calm; Peace

R

Reason
cure of illness by, 63, 95
developing the faculty of, 95
intuition and, 209, 210, 213
Receptivity
to adverse forces, 32
of the body, 45, 107, 158, 160-
62, 178, 219
for cure, 36, 45, 49, 100, 107,
219-20
to the divine Force and Consciousness, 156, 158-60, 166-
67, 203, 207, 219
lack of, 14-15, 17-18, 24, 184
psychic being and, 113-14
quietude and, 159-60

S

Sadhak
attitude of, in illness, 76, 83
medical treatment and, 187-88,
197
and the practice of medicine,
197-212 *passim*
yoga and, 156, 222-23
See also Yogi, yogin
Sanitation
diminishes natural power of resistance, 60
indispensable in ordinary life,

60-61
Skin diseases, 23
Sleep
control of the subconscient in,
72, 76
illness can enter during, 42
pain and, 98
quiet mind and, 103
Soul, *see* Psychic being
Spirit
all is a form of, 11
body is an instrument of, 11, 12,
91
as inner doctor, 190
opening to, 151
Spirituality
the old and the new, 4
Sri Aurobindo
cure of illness by, 203-4, 211
healing power of, 219, 222
use of the Force by, 11
Stomach pains, 115
Stories
of Coué, 80-82
Doctor R and use of the Force
in healing, 200-201
influenza epidemic in Japan, 32-
35
lady with falling hair, 81
medical officer and the cholera
epidemic, 59
the Scientist and the cobra, 65-
66
Yogi on the banks of the
Narmada, 23
Subconscient
changing the, 68-69, 85-86
control of, during sleep, 72, 76
defeatism of, 169
defined, 67-69

fear and illness, 54-55, 64
illness and, 40-42, 69-71, 82,
  168, 185, 197
imposing a will on, 76
influence on the body, 64, 67-
  68
mental suggestions and, 70, 82-
  83, 149
mind in, and illness, 41, 69-70
resistance to the Force, 168
Subtle body, *see* Nervous envelope
Subtle vital envelope, *see* Nervous
  envelope
Suffering
  finding the truth through, 232-
  36
  mastering, 135, 178-79
  reason for, 229-35
  unreality of, 235-36
Sunstroke, 99, 162-63
Supramental consciousness, 111
  absolute immunity and, 42-43
  bringing down, 11
  opening to, 148
Supramental force
  acts without conditions, 156
  body-mind is chief obstacle to,
  13
Supreme, the
  faith in, 146
  intervention of, 156, 177
  See also Divine, the; Divine
  Grace, etc.
Surrender
  of the cells, 178-79
  to the Divine, 25, 138, 176-79,
  225
  to the inner guidance, 214
  in yoga, 8, 142, 156

T

Tantra, 152
Tension
  in humanity, 3-4
  inner, and illness, 17-18
  relieving, 103, 161-62
Tetanus, 50
Toothache, teeth, 23, 26, 97, 134,
  221
Transformation
  action of the Force for, 14, 154,
  166
  and the body, 13-16, 133, 167,
  193
  and illness, 23, 83, 159, 170,
  177, 231
  yoga and, 8-9, 11, 14-16, 61,
  123

V

Vaccination
  confidence in, 59
Vibrations
  all is a perpetual play of, 30, 44,
  51, 158
  are contagious, 25, 30, 56, 60,
  230
  of harmony for cure, 25, 26, 39,
  59-60, 96, 142, 221
  of illness, 16, 43-44, 132-34,
  191
  of nervous envelope, 39, 43-44,
  46
Vital being/consciousness
  characteristics of, 200-201
  equilibrium of, 27, 46, 57
  faith of, 85, 146
  fear in, 56-58, 61, 64, 66

has its own consciousness, 125
and illness, 17, 24, 28-29, 37,
   50, 71, 76, 98, 164, 184, 219
mistreats the body, 127-30
and tension, 161-62
Vital beings/forces
and evolution, 4
and illness, 31-32, 34, 43
Vital body/envelope, *see* Nervous
   envelope
Vital mind
and illness, 41, 67

W

Will
of the body, and illness, 37, 87,
   129, 132
of the cells, and illness, 77, 129
control of fear by, 57
cultivating the, 78, 116, 121
defined, 77, 166
rejection of illness by, 42, 44-45,
   55, 75, 76, 87
and the subconscient, 76, 82
use of the Force and, 152, 159,
   205, 207, 217-18
use of, in illness, 59, 77-78, 106-
   7, 126, 184,
use of, in pain, 161
Will (divine)
body as instrument of, 12, 126
cells opening to, in pain, 94
is divine support of life, 189
doctor's reliance on, 197
faith in, 94, 142

individual will and, 76
surrender to, 25, 54, 57, 155,
   176-77, 178
World
action of the Force in, 154, 204,
   208, 230
is a cauldron of Medea, 5
Divine Grace working in, 150,
   225
is a play of forces, 198, 233-34
transformation of, 14, 15

Y

Yoga
all life is, 5, 7, 18
and the body, 11-16, 62, 125
defined, 5
evolution and, 1-9
fearlessness needed for, 57, 61,
   66
illness and, 14-19, 188
immunity from illness and, 71,
   83
in the modern world, 5-10
opening, surrender in, 142, 172
preparing oneself for, 9
and transformation, 8, 11, 14-
   16
and use of the Force, 156
Yoga-Shakti,152; *see also* Force
   (divine, spiritual)
Yogi, yogin, 7
and illness, 42, 62, 75, 98, 152,
   183
See also Sadhak